SEVEN GRASS HUTS:
*An Engineer's Wife in
Central-and-South America*

Books by

CECILE HULSE MATSCHAT

MEXICAN PLANTS

GARDEN CALENDAR

—

(GARDEN PRIMERS)

ANNUALS AND PERENNIALS

SHRUBS AND TREES

BULBS AND HOUSE PLANTS

PLANNING THE HOME GROUNDS

HOW TO MAKE A GARDEN

—

SUWANNEE RIVER:
Strange Green Land

SEVEN GRASS HUTS:
An Engineer's Wife in Central-and-South America

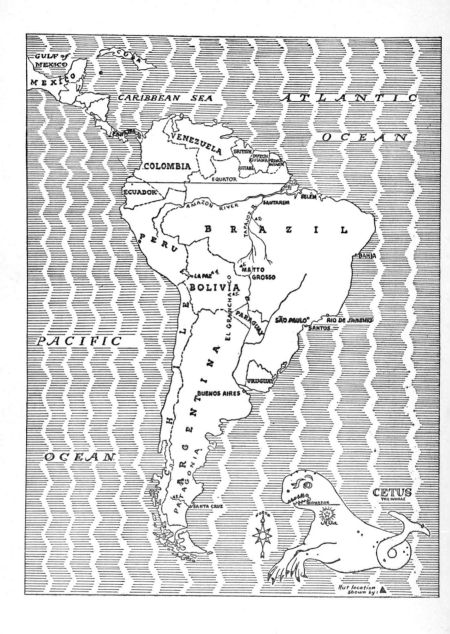

GULF of
MEXICO

MEXICO

CUBA

CARIBBEAN SEA

ATLANTIC

OCEAN

PANAMA

VENEZUELA

COLOMBIA

BRITISH
GUIANA

DUTCH
GUIANA

FRENCH
GUIANA

EQUATOR

ECUADOR

AMAZON RIVER

SANTAREM

BELÉM

P E R U

B R A Z I L

TAPAJOZ R.

A.2.

BAHIA

LA PAZ

A.4.

MATTO
GROSSO

BOLIVIA

A.5.

PACIFIC

EL GRAN CHACO

PARAGUAY

SÃO PAULO

RIO DE JANEIRO

SANTOS

C H I L E

A R G E N T I N A

URUGUAY

BUENOS AIRES

OCEAN

P A T A G O N I A

A.6.

SANTA CRUZ

NORTH

CETUS
THE WHALE

EQUATOR

Hut location
shown by :

SEVEN GRASS HUTS

An Engineer's Wife in Central-and-South America

BY

CECILE HULSE MATSCHAT

ILLUSTRATED WITH SKETCHES
BY THE AUTHOR AND
PHOTOGRAPHS

NEW YORK
The Literary Guild of America, Inc.

1939

TO

MY HUSBAND

CONTENTS

Chapter Thirteen

JAGUAR HUNT IN THE CHACO 212

Chapter Fourteen

THE DEATH GOD 235

Chapter Fifteen

THE LACONDONES POISONED TRAILS 243

LIST OF PHOTOGRAPHS

SEVEN GRASS HUTS:
An Engineer's Wife in
Central-and-South America

Chapter One

THE GAUCHO

*Matéo—Emily Post scratches in the courtyard—A
damn skinny woman—Three women, not wives—
The bride sets out with lacy lingerie*

THERE WERE PLENTY of huge men about, but none
that answered the Duke's description. "Look for the
biggest thing that walks," he said. "That will be
Matéo."

Matéo, an English-speaking Paraguayan gaucho
had been my husband's assistant on several engineering jobs in South America. They had traveled thousands of miles together. Yet, as I stood on the steps
of the train from São Paulo, I had no inkling as to
what his attitude toward me would be. I could not
know it would be months before he ceased to resent me.

The Duke had said nothing at Matéo's failure to
meet him. My husband was to make a rough layout
and inspection of large tracts of land along the frontier of civilization in Matto Grosso, northwest of

3

San Luis de Cáceres. He had notified Matéo to meet the train.

The trip upriver from Puerto Esperanço to Corumbá, an important Brazilian port on the west bank of the Paraguay, was short. Long before the boat docked, we saw a rocky ridge of limestone hills, upon which the city sprawls, lift skyward from the barren plains.

The wide, paved streets were shaded by low-spreading scarlet-flowered mimosas. As we followed our baggage to the hotel, past the one-story, well-built houses, the Duke kept a sharp lookout for Matéo.

The hotel was comfortable, a rambling building surrounding a patio. My husband went at once to take a pull shower, the greatest luxury the place afforded. We were covered with dust, terra roxa, the fertile red dust of Brazil which stains buildings, clothing, hair, and even skin an odd pinkish-red shade; in some parts of the country, rain turns the red earth to violet.

"The stone floor has just been washed, Senhor," said the dark-skinned servant proudly, leading the way to the shower, "and the water is clean." For years all the water for the city was drawn from a communal well; carts peddled the water from house to house and sold it by measure to the inhabitants. The Duke, from long experience, always inquired about the bath water. It was safer. In small hotels without baths or showers, peons often dip bath water direct from a pool or a river; it might contain anything from a tadpole to a small snake or an electric eel.

I was taking a rooster and two hens to my new home in Matto Grosso, the wildest, the least-known section of Brazil; not even Amazonia is so little understood. I fed the chickens and let them out to exercise. Their relief was equaled only by their good nature. Human beings incarcerated so would have scratched each others' eyes out. I like chickens. Brigham Young began at once to strut, Mae West to preen and groom her bosom—her style had been slightly cramped. Emily Post, with gallinaceous correctness, efficiently investigated the possibilities of the debris in the courtyard.

I was turning back to our room when I heard a commotion in the street. I rushed to the portal of the hotel. A heroic figure loomed in the archway. Horse and man appeared as one; they filled the air from sky to earth with a mountain of flesh. Huge spurs, fastened with rawhide thongs to horny, bare feet, clanked at every move of the jet-black stallion that stood on its hind legs and pawed the air with white forefeet, while the rider braced himself by tiny stirrups, large enough to accommodate only two or three of his toes. Agile as a jaguar, the gaucho dropped to the ground and walked lightly toward me with the rolling gait of a born horseman. He wore a bright red shirt and a brown leather apron. From his six-inch leather belt, equipped with "44" and cartridges, hung packets for tobacco, cigarettes,

money, candies, fishhooks, a rosary, and various
charms. My eyes, traveling down this giant of a
man, took in the tight-fitting white cotton trousers,
beneath loose leather leggings, which covered legs as
thick as posts—a drawstring confined at his ankles
the pants that reached almost to his armpits. As he

stopped beside me I could not take my fascinated
eyes from his belly, which waggled back and forth
like jelly before it "sets."

The Duke approached unheard and chuckled at
my astounded face. It had never dawned on me,
despite all he said, that such a monstrous man could
exist and live, not to mention work; three hundred

pounds would be a fair estimate of his weight. They greeted each other like old friends; no one could mistake the warmth of feeling between them. Matéo's sweeping black mustachios almost vanished in the nest of wrinkles that webbed his brown face; the great jowls that reached nearly to his shoulders quivered with emotion.

But there was nothing of affection in the beady black eyes that swept *me* from head to foot; my skinny frame, black hair, tanned skin, the keen eyes saw it all at a glance.

"This," said the Duke, "is the bride."

Matéo studied the "Senhora Boss" in silence. Finally he said abruptly, *"That* your woman?" His tone expressed complete unbelief.

"Holy cow's blood!" The gaucho shook his head in disgust. "Damn skinny woman!" He slapped an apology for a ten-gallon hat on his tangled black hair and stalked out.

I *thought* of a lot of things to say, but didn't. I *felt* like a rag without a bone and a hank of hair. The Duke, as usual, said nothing.

I feel certain, now, that Matéo never loved a woman, not as most of us know love. He boasted three women, not wives, and to him they were merely goods or chattels, fit only to work and to perform their natural functions. His women were hale and hearty peasants, none weighing less than one hundred and seventy pounds, short and squat, with broad flat faces and lank unwashed hair. Until brought together into a communal home, they were strangers, but they looked like triplets. They lived together near Asuncion in a whitewashed wattle-and-mud hut, palm-thatched, worked in the garden, made the weblike Paraguayan lace "wheels" and squares, and patiently awaited the infrequent visits of their master and the resultant visits of the stork.

Matéo gave his complete devotion to my husband and, because of it, he gave me loyalty. To him I was the "Senhora Boss," a hundred-pound weakness of the Duke's, as such to be guarded and cherished. "Every man," said he grandly, "is entitled to his failings. The Senhor Boss has only one."

This was the first of many trips. Some trips lasted only a few weeks, sometimes we were on location for months. The Duke's work in the States I have mentioned only casually. All the characters are portraits from life. None are creatures of imagination. Cities, towns, villages, and country are as I saw them. With the exception of large cities, change in Latin America is so gradual that the scenes of yesterday remain contemporary. No chronological sequence has been followed. This has permitted me to write of each country as a whole, rather than in fragmentary sketches. Most of the illustrations are taken from my sketchbooks.

Life, as I look back over the years, has been better than I dreamed. True, I often have been lonely. I

have stayed alone for months, working, studying, fill-
ing in the time as best I could. Whenever possible
I have shared my husband's adventures; then life—
in spite of hardships, of sickness, of danger—has been
a lark. I've seen uncharted jungles in Matto Grosso,
wind-swept pampas in Patagonia, and the sun rise
over snow-capped Cordilleras. I've houseboated on
the Paraguay, watched a jaguar hunt in the Chaco,
sung hymns to the skirling of a bagpipe, to please
a madman's whim in Amazonia, walked the Lacondones' poisoned trails, and been sent the Death God
in Panama. I've sat up all night with an Indian I
thought seriously ill; I gave him a sedative to ease
the pain, but in the morning I discovered all that
ailed him was a baby born to his wife the night before. I've had plenty of thrills, and no regrets. I
returned to the tropics each time with renewed interests, renewed enthusiasm; to me they are still the
gates to Paradise.

I set out alone from New York on my first trip to
join my husband in Cuba. But he was unable to
meet me there, after all; he wrote me at the hacienda
of friends, near Rodas, to come on to Brazil. Armed
with paints, water-color pads, and a trousseau of
lacy lingerie, it was a happy, if somewhat frightened
bride, that took passage from Havana on the old
Santa Rita, a reeking, coastal cargo boat—destination
Bahia, four thousand miles from home.

Chapter Two

THE BRIDE MET A STRANGER

Meet the Professor—"I'm asking you to marry me"—
The Minister and the garter snake—Engineers are
pioneers—Life on a cargo boat—Bed-loving snakes—
Bahia and a stranger

THE PROFESSOR ROLLED out of his berth again! His
maudlin voice rose loudly on the salty air . . .

"The bells of hell go ting-a-ling-a-ling,
    For you, but not for me."

The steward grinned; this was the third time he
had gone to the Professor's assistance since we left
Havana.

I could not resist laying my ear to the cabin wall.
I didn't want to miss anything. The Professor was
a darling in addition to being an entomologist from
Heidelberg. His doings were unpredictable.

He, too, had been a guest at the hacienda near
Rodas where I had waited for my husband. I will
always remember our first meeting. Across the cob-

bled courtyard, one evening, strode an extraordinary figure, short and tubby, from which emanated an aura of light and gauzy nets; a cloud of moths and other insects fluttered in the illuminated halo above his bald, pink pate. The point of largest circumference, his waist, appeared to be encircled by glittering, small windows; closer inspection proved them to be slender bottles filled with crawling bugs. In one hand this apparition clutched a lighted lantern, in the other an assortment of butterfly nets; a collecting jar was hugged under his arm. Blue, near-sighted eyes peered intently through old-fashioned steel-rimmed glasses perched on a snub red nose; a scraggly gray goatee stuck out at right angles.

". . . Ticks, *Ixodidae,* order *Acaridae,*" he mumbled as he passed. I noticed then that the halo above his head was caused by rays from his jack lamp, worn "bass-ackwards", which shone through a nimbus of scanty gray hair.

I was delighted the first day on board the *Santa Rita* to find that the Professor also had taken passage on the boat. In the intoxicating days that followed, he had opened up to me a vast and complicated world —the world of insect life. But now the voyage was almost over; it was our last day on board.

We were off the Brazilian coast, but Bahia, our final port of call, was still hours away. Five bells sounded; the repeat scudded by on the wind—6:30 of a stormy December morning. I went on deck, too excited to sleep longer. Elbows on the rail, body adjusted to the rise and fall, I watched the waves race away astern.

The old schooner sank her rail in the boiling seas as she forged steadily ahead against the storm blowing over us; she shook herself, swung back again to slap viciously at the angry rollers that reflected the inky clouds above. The broad, brown face of the Cuban helmsman at the wheel was tense.

I moved to a sheltered spot and pulled a robe around me. From the moment the ragged outlines of Cuba sank low on the horizon to this moment, so much had happened I'd had no time to think. Strange, how so many things happen to some people and so few things to others, how often small things change the pattern of our lives.

If it had not been for the letter, how different my life would have been. I did not need to see it. I knew by heart the contents of the single sheet of foreign bond. . . .

Sunday—noon
La Paz, Bolivia

Dear Cecile:

I finished the preliminary survey a week ago and we are celebrating here in La Paz, the highest city in South America.

As I write, the roses in the window pots are swaying in the breeze, but the mountains that seemingly climb from the end of the street are capped always with snow. You'd like it here!

I'm thinking of taking a job close to New York, say four or five thousand miles away, but if you can't see your way clear I guess I'll go out to Mesopotamia; I hear there is a dandy opening there. But I'd like it awfully if you'd think about it.

I'll be home about the twentieth.

Take care of yourself.

With love,

"The Duke"

P.S. On reading this over it occurred to me that perhaps I didn't make it quite clear that I'm asking you to marry me. I'll do better after I have some practice.

P.P.S. I'm enclosing a rose: it has an awfully nice smell.

I was a schoolgirl when first I met the Duke. Enthralled, I listened to his tales of buried treasure and lost cities. Then he went away. Occasionally I'd receive a card postmarked from some foreign place; it may have been from Iloilo or Cienfuegos or Shanghai—I don't remember, for he worked in all of these. When he returned it was as though he had never been away. I was so very happy. Then we quarreled, bitterly, as lovers often do; the reason doesn't matter. Time went on. I studied painting and told myself I would devote my life to art.

When his letter came I changed my mind. I never have been sorry.

Yet, had I won my first love, I might not have turned so ready an ear to an engineer's tales of far-away lands. It really began when the Minister's wife found a garter snake in his new silk hat. . . .

I was eight years old.

The Minister was young and handsome, with red hair and, if I remember correctly, a freckle or two. He was the first adult, aside from the members of my family, to pay attention to me as an individual. Although to him I was just a little girl with a liking for the things that were his hobbies—flowers, birds, beasts, and even reptiles—to me he was a god. We were pals. He taught me to box and we had many a grand battle until the pupil accidentally outboxed the teacher; he preached the following Sunday with a patch over one eye.

Life went along smoothly for nearly a year. Then came the night of the church supper.

The church in the little village up in the Wawayanda Hills of New York State usually was well-attended. All of the social activities were under the guidance of the Lord.

The strawberry festival had been held in June on the lawn of a church member who lived in the village; the corn roast in August had been at the home of a family living on the outskirts of town. The third event of the season was to be at our house in late October; after the supper all cakes and pies remaining would be raffled off, as was the custom, the proceeds to go toward the minister's salary.

The farm on which we lived was more beautiful than any other I have seen. A brook of running water crossed its meadows and spread out to form a pond where water lilies bloomed in summer. Woods and cattle pasture checkered the land between the plowed fields and, on the north, rising steeply from the pond's edge, was a heavy stand of almost virgin timber. Here all the birds of our community built nests. Swifts nested in the chimneys of our old white-pillared house and other birds sought shelter beneath the eaves of the red barns, in the corn cribs, in the old trees of the apple orchard, and in the wild plum and alder thickets along the brook.

No fairer day had ever dawned than that of the "Ladies Aiders'" supper. The smell of burning leaves drifted into the open windows of the kitchen where for a week the ordinary routine of the household had been upset by an orgy of cleaning and baking. My maternal grandmother, true to Dutch tradition, was noted for her cakes and pies; as for her homemade wines—blackberry, cherry bounce, rhubarb, and grape, pressed from frost grapes just beginning to burst their skins—the long row of empty bottles, which always stood in the pantry after any gathering, spoke volumes for their excellence. Perhaps I remember the bottles so clearly because I used to tiptoe softly down the row to drain the last drop from each one. I still think it was the sweetest wine I ever tasted.

All day the work went on. From time to time I

inspected the dining room where the tables, stretched
to their full length, were weighted with food—cakes,
baked beans with salt pork and molasses, platters of
chicken, turkey, and other cold meats, homemade
bread, the crust a soft, buttery golden-brown, pats of
yellow butter stamped with a clover leaf, pickles,
jellies, jams.

Before evening came, I thought the day would
never end. People gathered in the living room; I
peeked through the crack between the double doors.
The Minister stood in the center of the room and all
the people were crowded round, laughing and shaking
his hand. By his side was a tall, slim blond girl; she
was very pretty. She, too, was laughing and shaking
hands; occasionally he smiled down at her in a silly
fashion—or so I thought.

I pushed the doors open a little and whistled softly,
but the Minister paid no heed, although he had always
answered before. I had a present for him; my hands
shook and my breath choked me, I was so excited.
He would be pleased with this present, all right! I
had been taming it for weeks just for him.

Finally I went outdoors and crouched disconso-
lately beneath the open window. The Minister had
on clothes I had never seen before—a new suit and a
new silk hat. I scowled when I saw the girl, holding
his silk hat in her hand, simpering up at him. Gradually the crowd drifted closer to the window and I
caught fragments of their conversation . . . "and your

wife," I heard them say. Then I understood. He
had just been married. And he hadn't told me!

I was so hurt I felt sick. Suddenly I hated him.
He had treated me as a person and then had rele-
gated me to the status of a child. And I hated her,
too! I knew instinctively what would be her reaction
to the gift. I slid my arm across the sill and dropped

my present in the hat. The bride glanced down,
coyly, just as the garter snake slid its head over the
brim and gently flicked its red tongue against her
hand. She fainted.

Large plump ladies stood on chairs and held their
skirts high; little thin ladies draped themselves around
various objects. The Minister reached over, grabbed
me by the collar and pulled me halfway across the

window sill; then he delivered two hard smacks on an unmentionable place.

My pride was in tatters. I turned the incident over and over in my mind. I prayed that the garter snake looked to her as large as a boa constrictor. I refused to eat and the doctor prescribed a tonic, but I became thinner and thinner.

One day Uncle, of whom I was very fond, brought a friend of his to see me. He had just returned from the tropics and was the first engineer I had ever met. I listened entranced to his fascinating stories of the jungle. Soon I ran around as of old, but now all my thoughts were of engineers and bridges and roads in hot countries. I read everything I could get my hands on about the tropics; I neglected my studies and stern measures had to be taken to see that I knew something more than jungle lore.

The Minister and his wife moved to another parish. Years passed and the incident faded into the background of my thoughts. I went away to school; but my heart still was set on being an engineer. However, I discovered quickly that women cannot compete with men in engineering, especially in the tropics. I knew that I must find another way to solve my problem.

If I had not been so obsessed with the life of the jungle I might have married one of "the boys next door." Somehow I managed to get engaged to four of them; none of them took. Then I met another engineer and from the beginning I think I knew the end.

On sailing day I felt small and deserted and alone as I forced my way through the crowd on the Havana dock; some of them lugged chickens shut up in reed baskets; others hugged gamecocks, without which scarcely any native travels, to their sides. Near the entrance an old Negro, wearing a faded uniform cap with tarnished gold braid, leaned back in a rickety armchair.

"Passenger?" He spat accurately between the wide cracks of the floor boards. At my answering nod he led the way, and we catwalked up a short, steep gangplank, my guide boosting me from the rear.

The boat had all her cargo under hatch when I went aboard; rum, fertilizer, and cattle filled her hold to overflowing. She was a big, picturesque, trading schooner, square-sterned and squat, with patched, dingy-colored sails; on the stern was painted "*Santa Rita, Habana, Cuba.*"

Deck passengers were camped all over the best of the deck; their bulging bags and baskets were stowed beside them; fighting cocks were picketed safe distances apart. They were a happy crowd; a few had had too much to drink. Although slower than a liner, the schooner was infinitely more exciting. Even before we left port, cockfights and card games were in full swing; banjos twanged and voices hummed

constantly; a portly Negress shook the rumba with
a half-breed from Trinidad; ardent love-making,
primitive and convincing, went on to the accompaniment of the African drum, bamboula.

"Glad I took this boat," I assured myself, putting
away books and clothing. "The cockfights are sure
to be amusing." Chickens are in my blood. Always
at home I had a few of my very own; Dad developed
the Hulse strain of Rhode Island Reds, many of which
are Madison Square Garden prize winners. "Maybe
I'll do a little cockfighting myself," I thought. At
seven I had staged a marvelous cockfight in our barn
with two of Dad's prize-winning roosters, freshly
groomed for the county fair. Dad did not show
roosters that year. There was nothing left of the
winner. I chuckled to myself at the thought of it.

Still, I had a queer sinking feeling in the pit of
my stomach. Everything was so strange. Why, after
I had gone all the way to Cuba alone, didn't my husband meet me in Rodas, as we planned, instead of
insisting that I go on to Bahia? Chains rattled,
winches creaked, loud voices issued orders in an un-
familiar tongue. And the men—oily, smirking,
musky males—I, a young woman traveling alone
among Latins . . . I was tired, scared, miserable.
Whatever had possessed me?

With unsteady hands I hung clothing on nails
driven into the cabin walls. I thought of the Duke's
warning before our marriage. "It sounds exciting,
but it's a hard life," he said. "You've read too many

books; you're hoping for romantic adventures. They say no one ever finds adventure unless he takes it with him, but an engineer couldn't work that way, always keyed up; to us adventure is just part of the job. Civil engineers are really pioneers—we move from pillar to post, often only a few weeks in a place. If I were a mining man it wouldn't be so hard on you. They often stay with their families in one place for years."

"But look how long you were on the Amazon," I interrupted, thinking of his first job as a cub engineer; he worked on the final survey for the Madeira-Mamoré railroad in Brazil.

"That was a two-year contract," he admitted, "but no place to take a woman. You know the saying—a man died for every railroad tie spiked down. Much of my work is like that. If you marry me you must be content often with the bare necessities of life; sometimes you won't have those. You'll spend dreary days and weeks in furnished rooms; you'll eat badly cooked food, served worse. In the tropics you must housekeep in a tent, or in a palm-thatched hut where snakes live in the roof and three-inch cockroaches fall in the soup. Do you still think you'd like the life?"

"I certainly do," I replied promptly.

Yet the day I sailed on the *Santa Rita* I did not look ahead with so much joy. Before my eyes passed visions of a long, low comfortable room filled with happy, laughing people—my family. I discovered that talking of going alone to strange lands was one thing; actually to go was another. For one dreadful moment I was tempted to pack my bags and run. But the pull of affection was greater than my fears.

I stood at the porthole and watched historic spots pass to port and to starboard, as the dirty green water widened rapidly between boat and dock. On one hand was grim, weather-beaten Morro Castle; on the other the crumbling walls of the Castillo de la Fuerza.

It was in the morning that I came face to face with the Professor again, striding around the deck, his first drink of the day in one hand, in the other his butterfly net, prepared even in mid-seas for the itinerant butterfly. He had netted two migrating monarchs, he told me, on the trip down to Cuba. However, the only insect that came to the Professor's net on this trip was a superior two-inch cucaracha.

We called at Veracruz. This was Cortez' Rich Town of the True Cross, a picturesque mixture of old and of new. The harbor was beautiful, with its docks, its ships, and its zopilotes, the huge buzzards which are the accredited street cleaning department. The Professor and I were now very good friends. We went bathing; we nearly missed the boat, as we stopped to have our pictures taken.

We called at Trinidad. It was early morning. As we approached through the inside passage, the Golfo de Paria, the tiny islands seemed unreal. Three peaks stretch steeply upward from the palm-clad hills, the

"Three Sisters" which had inspired Columbus to call the islands after the Trinity. Port-of-Spain, the capital, looks theatrical because of its cosmopolitan population. The Professor and I did not go bathing— he wound wool on a little bobbin for his wife. She was tall, gaunt, devoted, and righteous. We did not have our pictures taken.

We called at Paramaribo. I did not go ashore. Foreign ports are not much fun when seen alone.

Those were lazy days; we ate, we slept, we fished for sharks, but I was never bored. The schooner, being of light draft, sailed so near the coast that land was almost always in sight. The boat rolled considerably, even though the weather was ideal, as the South Atlantic is never calm—trade winds sweep its waters. We were seldom alone. Other schooners passed and repassed, their white sails carrying them swiftly along in the path of the trades. "Fuel is expensive, wind is cheap," say the Latins.

I saw the red ball of the sun drop behind the jungle shores of Dutch Guiana; the lights dotted over three isolated rocks—Isles du Salut—popularly termed Devil's Island, although the name belongs only to one, the infamous French penal colony; the muddy yellow mouth of the river Oyapok, which pours its silt-laden waters into the blue Atlantic—below this natural boundary lies Brazil. I saw a million heat devils dance on a purgatory of dead trees, swamps, and uninhabited islands that stretch south of Cabo de Orange to the jungles of Amazonia; a white bird

flying low over the line where café-au-lait waters
from the Amazon meet the ocean's indigo-blue. I
heard the sacred bells of old Olinda, standing on its
palm-girt hill.

The fact that I was going into almost unknown
jungle country worried everybody but me; at least,
they all had a lot to say about it. I scarcely gave it
a thought.

"Did your husband warn you about the berne
flies?" asked the good Jesuit Father from Missiones
one night at dinner. "They sting right through your
clothes and lay eggs under your skin; little worms
hatch out."

It was too hot for soup.

"Be sure and tuck in your mosquito netting every
night," cautioned the Round-the-World-Traveler.
"That prevents the snakes from crawling in bed with
you. Why I know a man . . ."

It was too hot to eat at all. I left the table.

By the time I reached Bahia my mind was a confused jumble of worms, snakes, cannibal fish that ate
human beings, temperatures of 120 degrees in the
shade, savages that adored white girls but preferred
them fat . . . in short, I was prepared for the worst.

We came to Bahia at sunset. The storm had blown
itself out.

Houses slightly above sea level glided past. Red
roofs and glistening domes showed above the green

ridges. In my nostrils was the smell of salt water and
hot tar; in my ears was the sound of the flap-flap of
the awning. Suddenly a lighthouse appeared, surrounded by circular walls; the schooner sailed in a
great curve, turned to starboard, and entered the blue
immensity of the Bay of All Saints.

Bahia, built on a peninsula—sea on one side, bay
on the other—lay before us. It sprawled indolently,
mile after hazy mile, on wooded hills near the
equator.

Almost before the boat hove to, a tiny launch
put out from shore. Officials and other important
personages aboard were all in white. I scanned eag-
erly the faces of the dark-skinned men. I saw no
face I knew. Leaning over the rail, striving for a
clearer view, I scarcely saw the flock of canoes, with
their white, three-cornered sails, from which brown-
skinned men handed up green parrots and brown
monkeys. The boats were low in the water, loaded
with strange fruits: rosy mangoes, green avocados,
breadfruit, and mamão—a yellowish-pink tree melon
with a delicious orange-red pulp; there were many
others, of which I did not know the name. The sight
did not thrill me. I was interested in one thing only
—a familiar face—and I had not found it. Even
the Professor, my only real friend, had disappeared.

Men in white climbed up the ladder. My knees
shook and my hands were icy cold. Look as I might,
I saw no blue-serge-clad figure, such as I had seen
last on a liner's deck, and later watched through a

mist of tears until man and boat sank below the horizon.

Sick at heart I turned away. He had forgotten me already; probably a jungle woman—my ideas of jungle women were confused. Shouts of laughter! Someone grabbed me close, although I tried to jerk away. The captain, too, was laughing. A joke? I looked again at the man holding me—short, stocky figure, massive head, close-clipped black hair, keen black eyes, a mouth with laughter wrinkles at the corners. I looked again. The sun-blackened face beneath the white helmet looked familiar. It couldn't be. It was.

Shades of my good Dutch ancestors! The bride had come four thousand miles to meet a stranger.

Chapter Three

CAMILLA OF THE PAMPA

Sights of the city—The bridegroom is forgiven—
Strange food and a strange language—The market
place—Night in a honky-tonk—Black dancer with
red hair—Stalls of sin—The Professor and the
prostitute

I GREW UP in those few seconds I stood on the deck
of the *Santa Rita* and looked into the face of the
stranger who was my husband.

Some mysterious psychological change happened to
me as an individual when I married. I no longer belonged entirely to myself but was a part of somebody
else; and to that person I felt I was bound forever,
since to him I must return if I would be complete,
as persons torn by many loves can never be. Now
it seemed as though the warm, close, spiritual in-
timacy which tied us together was broken. Again,
I stood alone.

The Duke helped me down the ladder into the tiny
launch. As we chugged across the bay, the waters

27

glowed with a resplendent sheen from Nile blue to ultramarine, while wide streaks of emerald green cut the paler color. The side of the dock was wet and blackened by the encroaching tide.

The baggage turned up eventually under "H". While waiting, I watched the boats of all nations, dotted around the harbor, admiring the specks of white sails which appeared and disappeared in the far distance. Low ridges of hills nearly surround the immense bay and in many ways I think it more beautiful than that of Guanabara; the harbor of Rio is of course more dramatically, more startlingly, lovely, but it has not the old world charm, the poignant appeal of the Bay of All Saints.

The city was completely enchanting. Locally called São Salvador, the name Bahia being applied only to the state, the town is a double decker, like Natchez on the Mississippi. Lower town is a narrow strip of land at sea level; upper town, more than a hundred feet above, is on the plateau. American-built elevators carry the people from one level to the other, or they climb the steep streets or roads that wind around the cliffs. Houses—faded-pink, golden-tan, sky-blue, worn-crimson—cling closely to the hillside; they look friendly and inviting among dark trees.

A busy port, yet filled with the somnolence of too great an abundance of tropical nature. There seemed too much of everything. Already my French thrift, inherited from Dad, was up in arms at the apparent waste. People in white, often merely pajamas and slippers, strolled about the docks, the customs house, and the tree-filled praca, the square, in O Commercio, the lower town. Gigantic Negroes lugged bales of hides, bags of cocoa beans, tobacco, and cocoanuts from the warehouses to waiting lighters—the last three products are raised on the islands across the bay. Hundreds of shacks housed poverty—Negroes and soldiers of fortune whom luck has deserted. Weedy in mind, emaciated in body, they haunt the docks and beg from kindly tourists the price of a glass of native rum.

We drove slowly up the precipitous road to our hotel on the heights. Past us flowed an endless stream of people. Black or near-black women, smoking husky native cigars, were adorned with dozens of bracelets and neck ornaments of tin or wire or both; nearly all carried bundles on their heads. Many of them were swathed in heavy clinging flowered skirts, with red, yellow, or blue shawls, worn over sleeve-less camisoles, knotted under one armpit in the manner of their African relatives.

Walls towered above us—retaining walls, monastery walls, house walls. Among the crumbling pink stones of an old church a clump of blue-black aloes appeared tipped with frosty stars; a solitary century plant thrust its ivory spear of bloom above a pale-blue gate. I looked down upon walled-in gardens filled with crimson roses, purple bougainvillea, and scarlet tents of tuliplike flowers—flame trees in blossom, without leaves.

From our hotel window I could see the last slanting rays of the sun pour down upon low, distant hills. A little breeze wakened sleepy ripples on the smooth water of the bay; it rattled green, swordlike fronds on the royal palms.

"Tired?" asked the Duke apprehensively. He is beginning to regret the joke he played on me, I thought.

"Not much." I watched two sparrows quarreling in a jaboticaba tree—the blue-black fruits, about the size of a palm when mature, appear nailed to the trunk; it makes a good jelly, but a better wine.

"Sorry you came?" He moved closer. "You still can change your mind. But after we leave Campo Grande, a thousand miles from São Paulo, you can't turn back. I doubt if there's ever been a white woman where we're going; there's nothing there—no stores, no houses, no people—just jungle, and all the things that creep and crawl and fly."

The sparrows were a noisy pair.

"We'd have a swell time," remarked a casual voice beside me. Oh, how artful! "Game?"

I nodded. The sparrows were quiet now, close together on a limb.

The Duke put his arms around me, gently. I wasn't lonely any more. We stood there, not talking, and watched the last light die. The horizon was pale-green; in the sky floated purple and white clouds. Lights flashed from a million windows in the city. A sparkling cross was kindled on the bluff. For cen-

Upper: An Aztec Indian, the author, and a burro—"His-father's-name-Juanita." *Lower:* Covered boats are used on many Brazilian rivers, especially the Amazon and its tributaries. Entire families, often with no permanent homes, live on such craft.

Upper: Much of Latin America's traffic is by river or coastal launch—with livestock and human beings traveling on the same boat. *Lower:* A typical waterfront scene at Bahia.

turies before electricity, flaming reeds blazed this symbol on the hillside, the torch of faith.

Brilliant light poured through the diagonal blue slats of our shutters. I stretched lazily, luxuriating in the feeling of being stationary once more. From the heat I knew it was nearly noon. Suddenly I remembered that this was my first day in a Brazilian city. Rushing to the window, I peeked out.

Glittering white clouds hung motionless in a hot sky and were reflected in the blue flood of the bay. Huge trucks, piled with meat fresh from the slaughterhouse, snorted up the road; a wheezing matron with a basket of green and orange melons dropped the least of coins, the ancient vintem, in a drunken beggar's palm—he smiled and closed his dirty torn garment across his hairy chest; a pasty-faced clerk, pink shirt tucked into blue-checked pants, sloshed water over a blue-and-white tiled shopfront. Music; an archbishop, in a brocaded robe which swept the dust, walked under a gilt-and-purple canopy hung round with lace; fat monks in brown—brown beards, brown robes, brown sandals; a young seriema, a large, red-legged cranelike bird—yellowish-gray and brown—stalked with measured tread before the São João, imperial theater when Portuguese viceroys ruled the land; at intervals it uttered a shrill, piercing cry, then tilted its crested head as though listening for an answer from the wilderness, the Sertão whence it came.

The Duke smiled at me cheerfully; mosquito netting made minute purple crossbars on his face. A knock at the door and a black girl came in, carrying a brazier and two tiny coffee cups on a crimson tray. She strained the liquid through an oily blackened cloth; the drink was fragrant, thick, delicious—a potent eye opener.

We breakfasted at a terrace café overlooking lower town; in the bay a hundred feet below, small boats clustered around a silver schooner with patched sails; across the roadstead, now a brilliant green, sped gently heeling sailboats. The Professor and his wife, and the Round-the-World-Traveler also ate at the café. Mrs. Professor eyed me with a jaundiced eye; she still disapproved of cockfights and of picture taking, even though I, too, now wore a husband on my sleeve.

I wanted to explore immediately the hot narrow side streets and the countless pracas, dotted with squat palms, but the Duke handed me a menu and insisted that I eat first; the menu was in Portuguese, the language of Brazil. Even today my linguistic accomplishments are practically nil; that morning my sole knowledge of Portuguese consisted of two words. Bom dia, good morning, I repeated over and over like a parrot. The Duke speaks three languages well and has a working knowledge of three more; my refusal to bother with verbs and the like annoys him. I pick up a collection of phrases in many tongues, hook

them together, wave my arms, smile, and proceed
happily on my way. I don't recommend the method,
but it works, with variations. In all large Latin-
American cities, at least a few people speak a little
English.

The Duke ordered his meal swiftly and efficiently,
as did the other *Santa Rita* passengers. I took my time
and without help chose odd-looking items from the
menu by the simple method of pointing at them.
Sonho do Ouro, golden dream, was an orange on a
stick, its delicate skin peeled back like the petals of
a flower. Encouraged, I tried creme de abacate—it
turned out to be mashed alligator pear with sugar and
lime juice; served ice-cold it is a wonderful dinner
dessert, not so good for breakfast. Vatapá, much to
everyone's delight, would have fed a family of five, let
alone a portion for one small woman—it is meat or
fish, shrimps, coconuts, red peppers, spices, and mandioca flour, cooked together in palm oil. I gave up
and ate hot pan rolls and butter, with coffee.

Mrs. Professor went to take a nap; the Duke went
to finish an estimate; the Round-the-World-Traveler,
the Professor, and I went exploring separately. The
Professor was on the hunt for one of the most prized
of South American butterflies, the *Morpho bahiana*—
the loveliest in the world it is said; as lovely as the
little state for which it is named. Its rare beauty is
its doom. Its metallic-blue wings are sacrificed for
lockets, for trays, and even for table tops, and, unless

stringent laws are made soon and kept, the morphos
are likely to become extinct.

"It a disgrace iss," fumed the Professor. "Some of
the birds of Brazil protected are, but my peau-ti-full
morpho, its wings in every dirty leetle shop are peddled. I go."

He went.

Markets fascinate me. Upper town could wait, I

decided and took the elevator to O Commercio, where
huge blacks, male and female, loll in the shade hour
after hour in the hope of selling a penny's worth of
passion fruits or other exotic delicacies. I never saw
so many Negroes, not even in Southern cities in the
States. Once the center of Portuguese-America's
slave trade, more than three-quarters of Bahia's 346,-
ooo peoples are black; formerly the capital, the city
now is fourth in size.

For nearly two hours I sauntered through the

market place, crammed with all the fruits of the country except those native only to the torrid regions. Many of them I had never seen before, so I bought some of each to show my husband. I offered them a small copper vintem in payment and if they indicated that this twenty-reis piece was not enough, I gave them two. Arms filled to overflowing, I went back to the hotel, followed by droves of excited blacks, chattering and gesticulating about me. Fearful that I had broken some stringent law, I hurried to find the Duke. I remembered his description of a night in jail, during one of the revolutions; it did not appeal to me. However, I had merely violated an old Portuguese custom by carrying the fruit; in future I never carried so much as a new handkerchief; a servant walked behind me laden with the package.

Mangoes I liked. I held up an especially large pink and yellow specimen for the Duke's approval.

"Be careful how you eat those," he warned with a grin. "They say in Brazil you must never drink milk or liquor after eating mangoes or mangas, as they call them; they will poison you." South America is filled with such superstitions.

"What's this?" Ignoring his levity I held up a bright-green, prickly fruit, large as a melon.

"That's a jaca, a jack fruit. It grows directly from the trunk or bough. No stem." He cut it open to show the coarse pulp which surrounds the kidney-shaped kernels. The meat was sweet and very aromatic; the Negroes thrive on it. "This is a small one," he continued. "A single fruit often weighs thirty pounds. The tree was brought to Brazil from India the middle of the seventeenth century."

One by one he named the different fruits: sapotes, many kinds of bananas, custard apples—fructa de conde—whose soft pulp is eaten with a spoon, papaw or mamão, which is much like our cantaloupe or melon. The papaw, also called papaya throughout the tropics, is one of the most common, as well as the most useful, of fruits. The immense leaves are used in place of soap; tough meat, wrapped in the leaves and cooked, becomes very tender. Breadfruit, frutta pão, picked green, sliced and fried, makes an excellent substitute for bread; the white pulp has been for centuries the chief food of the Polynesians.

We went for a walk at twilight. Above the quiet of the bay a blue-white star peered forth. A liner was putting out to sea; its lights sparkled in the black water like molten gold, brown smoke belched from its funnels and a faint bronze stain remained against the cool green-yellow of the sky.

The top of the plateau is thickly settled, its streets crisscrossing in every direction. To the Duke, with his dislike of cities and crowds, it was an old story. To me the lights, the dark faces, the strange language —musical, with a metallic undertone—the hot, spiced food, went to my head like wine. Would I ever get enough of it?

Stores, hotels, theaters, churches—legend claims one for every day in the year, by actual count they probably total a hundred. Many of them are only pictureque ruins, but there are dozens of the massive colonial ones in use, with lovely old gardens and magnificent views; monasteries are plentiful, built in choice spots overlooking the bay or the sea, and crowded with fat monks.

It was Saturday night. Everything was very gay. Crowds, in from the suburbs for a night in town, jostled about, drinking, laughing, fighting, all in fun. The narrow streets were brightly lighted. Once we passed an open door, like an eye in the wall; from the garden beyond came the scent of dying flowers, the smell of rotting fruits.

We dined in a native honky-tonk. The Duke was worried. "It's cheap, vulgar," he protested, "not safe." But tomorrow we were sailing for São Paulo and his work. I couldn't bear to be cheated of the tiniest bit of life. I was afraid to go, but I couldn't stay away. We went.

The low, ramshackle building was of mud—red, like the Brazilian earth. Tall red candles, stuck in tins, burned fitfully; they cast deep shadows in the corners of the long room, flickered over the smoke-blackened eaves, and glinted on the shiny dirt floor. Occasionally the door of a brightly lighted room in back opened and light shone on dark faces and gaudy clothes. Rows of Negro men lined the walls. A few planters, a couple of German salesmen, a half-dozen sailors on a spree, sat around tiny bare tables eating and drinking.

Fumes of raw tobacco and rawer rum hung heavy in the air; mingled with it was the tang of gin tonica, favorite drink of the native women. A Negress with a narrow, childlike countenance, tiny piglike eyes and straight black bangs, proudly passed the drink around in an American mustache cup; "To My Sweetheart" was stenciled in gilt letters round the edge.

An old Negro, blind eyes deep-sunken, skin tight and polished like bone itself, twanged a few chords on a guitar. A slim, gypsyish girl, oval face the color of old ivory, smooth golden throat encircled with strings of scarlet seeds, crouched on her haunches at his feet and sang, as though to herself, a strange monotonous tune. Her voice was shrill and quavered a little, but still the wailing melody, broken by strange intervals, went on and on. In Bahia these popular ballads are a mixture of the medieval folk ballads of Portugal, combined with weird half-savage rites of primitive Africa. I was so entranced I almost forgot to eat.

The food was tempting. For the first time I ate the national dish, feijoada completa, with mandioca flour sprinkled over the black stew until it became white and thick as mush. Floury black beans, feijoa preto, are the base for this dish; in Bahia it is cooked with carne do sol, meat dried in the sun, but in other localities tongue, pork, sausage, or bacon, with spices, is added. Mandioca meal or farinha is derived from a Brazilian plant, the manioc or bitter cassava, which belongs to the poisonous Euphorbias; starch extracted from manioc is the tapioca of commerce. Centuries ago the Indians discovered that roasting the huge tubers of the cassava would remove the poison, hydrocyanic acid. White people profited by their experience and produced tapioca, but I prefer the real native farinha.

The singing stopped. Then the music started again, a different tempo, wild and stirring. A rough board, crudely lettered read: "Camilla of the Pampa." She apparently was a great favorite; they paid her the tribute of silence.

A girl whirled through a tiny door in the wall. She spun on her crimson slippered toes like a dervish, then stamped, looked contemptuously at the men lined against the walls and surveyed coldly the elite seated at the tables. Black, naked, except for a crimson skirt hung from a belt around her slender waist, she slowly extended long arms, fingers curled in strange mystic shapes, tremors rippled snakelike down her slim, emaciated body. Light, orange-red hair clung in tight curls to her small skull. Head tipped back, eyes half-closed, she swayed to the music; big brass earrings swung against her long dark throat. Softly, from some unseen spot, a drum began to beat, thudding in an unvarying monotone—never higher, never lower —on and on the rhythm pulsed through the hot darkness until the room was filled with savagery. Hips,

arms, body writhing, the girl bent backwards until
red curls touched black skin; tiny tip-tilted breasts,
crimson rouge smeared thickly on hard berrylike
nipples, stretched taut. She whirled faster and faster;
the full skirt stood away from her bare body like a
crimson flame. Sweat poured down her face, enormous nostrils in her flat nose distended, pale Negroid
lips curled back from white teeth. The great drum
boomed . . . louder, louder . . . a furious, rolling
crescendo. . . . The crowd leaned forward, tense, ex-
pectant. I could hear the sound of their labored
breathing; lust, desire, held them captive. Slower
moved the spinning figure . . . slower still . . . she
dropped to the floor . . . rose . . . sank again . . . was
gone.

Early Sunday morning I went for a walk. The
Duke was still asleep, but I was restless, excited by
the strange land I already liked so well. I wandered
down a street, stopping occasionally to admire some
colorful crowd on their way to market. A man and
two women were especially intriguing—they carried
on their heads large baskets packed with live chickens, legs up like a helpless turtle.

As I turned a corner I found myself in a soft-earth
lane that ran through dense bush to a green valley
dotted with clusters of Negro huts; even within the
city limits there are many of these seemingly rural
spots. The huts were small, one room, with little fur-

niture—a hammock, a chair, a rickety table. A long,
slender arm of the bay reached into the valley, cool
and quiet. Green grass ran down to golden sand. Over
the huts were twined and twisted wine-red bougainvillea; gold and white and lilac orchids perched on
trees. Men and women swung idly in hammocks slung
beneath the mangoes, whose dense crowns afforded
welcome shade. Breadfruit, alligator pears, and other
tropic fruits were theirs for the picking. With all
those things before them they felt no need of palaces,
of furniture, or wealth.

A girl of eight or so herded the young fry to the
inlet and poured water from a painted gourd over
their shiny plump bodies. One tiny tot escaped her
clutching hand; protruding tummy thrust out, he
paraded up and down before an admiring audience—
all the younger children had enormous banana bellies.

Watching, I laughed aloud at a vivid mental picture
of another child—a white child in a distant land—
that at three walked stark-naked down the main
street of her native town; they say I stopped often
to shake hands and to greet politely all my parents'
friends. That night I went supperless to bed. At the
sound of laughter, black faces turned my way; a
few tolerant of the white Senhora, most indignant.
Bahianas resent intrusion.

Back in the city I decided to stay out a while
longer. No doubt, I assured myself, the Duke is still
asleep; a pity to wake him. I sauntered along Rua
Victoria out to the old lighthouse and fort. The stone
benches scattered over the sloping greensward were
all occupied. Most of the couples were of the lower
class, but a few serious students read ponderous tomes
while other persons watched gannets drop plummet-
like into the sea.

The sun cast no shadow when I started back. I took
a short cut, thinking the Duke might worry as I had
been gone a long time. But somehow—just how I
never knew—I found myself in a strange but colorful
street, gay, well-kept, the street of alien prostitutes.
The Duke had said never to go down that street, but
it was only a couple of blocks from the hotel and I
was already there. . . .

I walked slowly and took a good look down into
each of the tiny stall-like apartments; the "cages" in
this particular block were about two feet below the
sidewalk. They were plainly furnished—two chairs,

a stand with a pitcher in either pink or blue, a bed in an alcove screened with curtains. The girls were extremely elegant; all types, all kinds. I had supposed they would look like a different race, but they appeared just like anybody else. I was bitterly disappointed.

Suddenly I stopped. Through a crack in sagging, broken blinds I could see into a narrow room. There I glimpsed a familiar figure. I rubbed my eyes and looked again. There was no mistake. Net in hand, it ran rapidly around the room, closely pursuing a broad-faced Amazonas female, clad only, so far as I could see, in a blue satin kimona and feather-trimmed mules with high gilt heels.

Chapter Four

POOR BUTTERFLY

Rescue of the Professor—Camilla, sweetheart of bandito—Down to Santos—Mae West invades our cabin

THAT SUNDAY I stood a long time in the hot street, undecided, wondering what to do. It wasn't, definitely, my affair. I thought uneasily of the Duke; he disliked interference in other people's business. "That," he once said unkindly, "accounts for your nose."

But I adored the Professor; he was so childlike. Something had to be done.

"Professor," I called. "Come right out of there. Suppose your wife sees you!"

That stopped the performance. But only for a moment. "*Morpho bahiana,*" he panted despairingly. Once more the chase began. But it became apparent now that it was the woman who was chasing the Professor. Over went the pink pitcher; the chairs followed suit. Howls of rage from the female. Heads

44

appeared at windows all down the block. It must
have been quite an unusual spectacle.

A hand shoved me aside. "Me, I get," said an im-
perious voice. Camilla, red head high, strode past.

"Loco! Loco!" screamed the frightened woman in
the cage of sin. I heard the smack of hand on flesh,
the voice of authority, and the wails and sobs changed
to sniffles.

One eye to the crack, the other watching the
street, I saw a stocky red-faced individual crawl
slowly backward from under the bed. Held tightly,
yet tenderly, between two pudgy fingers, the Professor clutched his *Morpho bahiana*—a painted insect in a street of painted women. Gently Camilla
touched the blue-metallic wings, edged with their
characteristic mourning band of black.

"Poor butterfly," she said. A shadow fell across her
face—fear, sadness, heartbreak?

Sheepishly the Professor started for the door. The
red head pointed to the broken pitcher. The Professor laid a milreis on the stand.

Convulsed with laughter, I leaned helplessly against
the wall. A flicker of mirth twitched the wide mouth,
innocent of rouge, as Camilla herded the Professor to
the street. We followed silently as he marched down
the walk, chin in air; injured dignity radiated from
his every pore.

Later I came to realize how little anything meant
to the Professor except his work; during the excitement of a bug chase everything else took second

place, in most instances nothing else existed. When field artist, later, for one of his expeditions in Central America I have seen him, time and again, literally crawl on his tummy through fetid mangrove swamps, while snakes and alligators slid aside at his approach. How he escaped being bitten I never knew. The prize usually was some measly, moth-eaten insect I wouldn't give houseroom. Of such caliber are scientists. More power to them!

When we reached the corner I grabbed his sleeve. "Wait," I begged. There was something I had to know.

"Who taught you English?" I asked the girl.

She smiled a tired, wise smile. "Sailormen, salesmen, all mens. Rio, Buenos Aires, everywhere." She opened her arms wide.

I was sorry I had asked.

"Me from pampas. I sweetheart bandito."

Bandit. This was life with a capital L. "Aren't you scared?"

She shrugged a Latin shrug. "He good so long he like; then he cut out tongue, cut ears, cut throat . . . so . . ." She drew a slim finger across her neck. A twinkle in the keen black eyes. "He ver' jealous." A quick glance at the Professor. "Ver' dangerous."

The Professor started off at a rapid trot. He looked slightly green. The sun, I thought. We covered the couple of blocks to the hotel in silence, each busy with his own thoughts. The Duke would be mad as hops, I knew. I'd been gone for hours.

From the street, no indication is given of the magnificent gardens enclosed by foot-thick house walls. The flat roofs are used as "penthouse" gardens, where the family sits each evening to enjoy the cool breeze and the sights of the town.

Tropical jungle through which all trails must be cut with a machete. So luxuriant is the growth that only a few weeks is sufficient to completely obliterate all signs of passage.

"Hmmmm!" The Professor cleared his throat nervously. "Hot," he puffed, wiping his bald dome. I said nothing.

He hesitated at the entrance, took off his specs, polished them briskly with a piece of toilet paper he carried especially for the purpose, squinted through them against the light; apparently satisfied, he pushed the steel bows over his ears, then regarded me owlishly. I said nothing.

Finally. "My wife . . . er . . ." he stammered.

"Too late, Professor," said I wickedly and pushed past him up the stairs to make my peace.

From our deck chairs on the flat roof of the saloon we watched the fading lights of the city. I begged to stay until the last of Bahia dropped below the horizon.

We were aboard one of the Brazilian costeiras— clean, comfortable coasting steamers that put into all the shallow lagoons along the coast of the southern states. After the hustle and bustle of sorting baggage and last-minute errands, the cool and quiet of the tropical night had never seemed more welcome.

It had been so hot on the deck, waiting, just before we sailed. The song of a thrush, the chestnut-colored sabia, had filled the air with poignant melancholy; the song, so wild, so sweet, like that of thrushes of northern lands, reminded me of home and family, thousands of miles away.

Partings, even from chance acquaintances, carry
with them something of sadness, of regret, of nostal-
gia. So, as I said good-by to the Professor, I discovered
the meaning of saudade, the most beautiful word in
the Portuguese language, for no other word so well
expresses all of these.

A moon rode slowly through the sky, a pale baby
moon, that seemed cut from cellophane. A star appeared, another, another, until the sky was spangled
with their twinkling lights. The city now was dim.
"Let's go below. I'm hungry," said the Duke. But I
hung back. I was in a panic because of what awaited
us in our stateroom.

But the moment could no longer be postponed.
The Duke steered me firmly below. Even before he
inserted the key in the stateroom door we were
greeted by strange sounds—scratchings, soft scurry-
ings.

The Duke looked at me questioningly. I swallowed
a funny sort of a lump, but said nothing. He threw
open the door, thrust his head around the jamb and
peered within. The storm lantern with which each
cabin was equipped had been left lighted; its dim
radiance shone upon my present, the basket standing
on the floor, with the Professor's card upon it. A
thoughtful bribe. But the lid was off. Our cabin had
turned into a chicken coop. On the top berth a pout-
ing cock with bright red comb and superior wattles
was pursued by a bold and chesty hen. From the lowest part of the commode issued a plaintive and sickly

clucking. The place seemed full of chickens. They
had taken possession! On the curtain rod before the
wardrobe a sleek and self-contained pampas beauty
was grooming herself. She stopped decorously to greet
us with an operatic series of cluck-cluck-adoos.

Disapproval sat glumly on the Duke's brow. He
glanced at the upper berth. "Brigham Young certainly knows his Mae West," he observed drily.

"Brigham Young, Mae West!" I laughed. After all
my trouble, I was not going to be defeated.

"What do you plan to do with this menagerie?"

"Keep them, of course." It had cost me a whole
milreis to smuggle them on board.

The plump pampas beauty, fluffing her oversize
bosom, fluttered down onto *my* pillow. The little
hen in the commode clucked admonishingly as she
scratched around to locate herself for the night.
"Lydia Pinkham," said the Duke slyly, "seems like
a sad female."

I was relieved by his apparent acceptance of my
contraband; at least, he had not said I couldn't keep
them.

"What shall we call that one up there?" The pampas hen took off from the curtain rod and lit on the
Duke's shoulder with a welcoming cluck.

He laughed in spite of himself. "She has the good
manners to make us feel at home," he said as he
brushed off his coat.

"Brigham Young, Mae West, Lydia Pinkham . . .
Emily Post," I said chuckling. Our family was com-

plete. They were to beguile many a tense moment and to furnish us with many an egg—except Brigham, of course.

MAE　　　　BRIGHAM　　LYDIA　　　EMILY

Chapter Five

AN ENGINEER'S HEADACHE

*Steamboat on the Paraguay—An engineer's problem
—Santos—"Road of Golden Rails"—Death of Lydia
Pinkham—I never saw the snake farm—A surprise
for the Duke—Matéo and Onca—Days on a river
boat—My first Indians—Birds and animals along the
upper Paraguay—Adventure with cannibal fish—
Paddling up a jungle river—The Duke's headache—
Green Hell*

LATE ONE AFTERNOON in January a small steamer
cast off her moorings from the Corumbá landing and
threaded her way along the winding palm-fringed
Paraguay. She moved slowly, pulling an added
burden, a barge loaded with horses and pack oxen.
The Duke had intended purchasing these at San Luis
de Cáceres, but Matéo objected. They might be hard
to secure there, he said.

The Duke took Matéo's advice. He was very anxious to have the job run smoothly and rapidly, as he
preferred this type of work and hoped to secure more

51

commissions like it, where he was on his own and could use his own initiative. Most of his jobs were preliminary surveys or construction work for large companies, such as International Paper, White, Du Pont, Habana Central, Empire Engineering, the Mc-Cormick interests, and various firms of consulting engineers. But occasionally he reconnoitered the field for individuals like Tex Rickard, who bought large tracts of land in the Gran Chaco for cattle raising. His client here was a wealthy Brazilian who dreamed of repeating Rickard's experiment in Matto Grosso.

I was in high feather. The air was cool and fresh on the river, and I bustled about my unpacking with a light heart. The week's trip to Cáceres, which might have bored persons less interested in the country and its beauties, seemed to me a gift from the gods.

All the way from Bahia to Santos I had been seasick; the coastal steamers, flat-bottomed and practically keelless, rock frightfully at all times. I remained in bed, even in the harbors. All I saw of Rio was the glittering strings of lights of the Avenida Atlantica, which every night flood Copacabana's promenade in a scintillating blaze. I cried, I was so infuriated. The Duke said not to mind, we'd see all the sights on our return.

We rushed through Santos, the great coffee port of São Paulo, so quickly I had only a glimpse of the city with its long strings of docks and warehouses. Brazil produces more coffee than any other country in the world; at least half of the crop is grown in the state of São Paulo. Long before we docked, the aroma of roasting coffee came over the water; a delicious volatile oil, air-borne, a delicate fragrance such as we in the northern hemisphere seldom may enjoy. Coffee for export is shipped unroasted.

All else that I remember about Santos is that the beach seemed alive with great birds the size of turkeys—urubús or vultures, locally called "Old Johns", hunting their breakfast of dead fish or other booty cast up by the sea. The sun glinted on their outspread wings and corpulent black bodies. Vultures are a common sight in the interior as well as along the coast. I have watched them congregate like ghouls around a wounded animal, their evil eyes watching every twitch of its misery, and, if birds can think, probably wondering how soon it would die.

The Duke had business in São Paulo, the capital of the state of that name, otherwise we would have taken the train for Puerto Esperanço from Rio. São Paulo stands on a plateau at approximately 2,500 feet. The fifty-mile broad-gauge mountain railroad leading up to it, the Duke said, was an engineering feat of gigantic proportions; it is called "The Road of Golden Rails" because it cost so much to construct.

I never questioned his statement as to the difficulties of surmounting a climb of over 2,500 feet, up sheer cliffs, in six or seven miles; nor did I deny the ingenuity with which the British engineers built the cableway, as the switchback principle employed by Meiggs on the Oroya Railway in the Peruvian Andes was impossible. My husband was so absorbed with the odd little engine, whose chief function seemed to be to hook the cars to the cable, that he paid no attention to the magnificent view. But I refused to be enthusiastic over what looked to me like a glorified elevator. I thought the scenery was stupendous.

Cubatao and Pissaguera are little towns in the banana and pineapple plantation districts; almost from the very edge of the cultivated lands the sierra rises abruptly to the abertura, the pass in the mountain range at Alta da Serra. It was my first trip through real tropical jungle and the most enchanting thing about it was the unreal color of the light—a weird pale green—like sunlight filtered through water. Parrots screamed, monkeys chattered and chirred. Trees were gardens of blossoms—red, blue, yellow, white, I never learned their names. Long creepers dropped tentacles from every bough; a special patrol is always on the lookout so that vines do not fall upon or loop across the tracks.

I didn't see how one train could pass another, as the track had only three rails. At the halfway point, however, the track broadened to four rails. Trains always pass here, as they work by a "balance of power" system. The five table inclines are broken by short stretches of slope between; each incline is about a mile long.

At Alta da Serra we had a short wait before finishing our run over the grassy slope to São Paulo, Brazil's second city in size; roads and bare banks showed blood-red against the green. Treetops, covered with exotic orchids, reared their heads from the pale clouds of mist that billowed and drifted across the world spread out below; waterfalls sprayed pearl-like drops upon flowers and birds near by. For the first time I realized the immensity of this man-made railway. No elevator this, but an awe-inspiring spectacle second to none, even if it was intended in the beginning, as a freight railway to carry millions of bags of coffee. I shuddered at the thought of what would happen if the cables should break, though every safety device possible has been added.

I looked at the chickens and gave them a drink. Brigham and the two hens with him were in splendid condition, but Lydia Pinkham seemed droopier than ever; she refused to eat or drink. I had been worried about her for days and wished I had a pink pill to give her, the same kind that we always put in the chickens' drinking water back home.

The Duke was cross because I fussed over the chickens and did not rest; the air was cool and pleasant after the heat of the jungle. As soon as we reached the railway station, the Estado da Luz, in São Paulo, I looked in Lydia's basket. She was lying on her back, alas, her small yellow feet upturned. I gave the porter a milreis to see that she had a decent burial.

While the Duke was busy I sat in a park, the Garden of Light, which forms an admirable waiting room for the city's great railway station, or drove around the wide modern boulevards and admired the buildings; the business streets were older—narrow and crooked—and traffic is, of course, congested.

The most interesting building in São Paulo, to me, was the Ypiranga Museum, standing on a little hill where Dom Pedro first proclaimed Brazil's independence from Portugal. After seeing the splendid collections of beija-flores, kiss-flowers or hummingbirds, and pica-paos, pick-sticks or woodpeckers, I went to the stationery store and laid in a large supply of pencils and notebooks. The bird life in Brazil, to say nothing of the flowers and insects, is almost unbelievable.

I am undoubtedly the one person in the world who has visited São Paulo and not seen the Butantan snake farm. I console myself with the reflection that one cannot see everything, but it is poor comfort. I like snakes almost as well as chickens. The Instituto Serumtherapico is one of the most remarkable institutions in the world. Its founder, Dr. Vital Brazil, has prepared three serums to act as antidotes for the bites of poisonous snakes—one for the Bothrops group, to which the fer-de-lance and the bushmaster belong, another for the Cascabel or rattler group, and a third for general use when the identity of the snake is in doubt. The Duke bought sufficient serum for our party.

The train ride across the continent had been long and tiresome. Campo Grande, with its wide red streets, sidewalk cafés, and cosmopolitan population —Portuguese, Italian, Japanese, Indian, Negro and half-breeds—was interesting; but, hot and dusty as it was, Corumbá had seemed like paradise. I was glad when we reached the end of the journey and started up the Paraguay; we had traveled so many, many miles. I wanted a home of my own. After all, I was still a bride and I had never had a chance to use my grandmother's wedding silver which I carried with me in the bottom of my trunk. I had also purchased an adorable set of native pottery in the Corumbá market.

The Duke did not know it. I could hardly wait to surprise him. Our first home would be in the far reaches of the Matto Grosso, almost at the foot of the high plain, the Plan Alto. What would it be like?

A broad-beamed, tubby little boat, the *Dom Pedro*, took us up the Paraguay. She was an old two-decker, painted white, with a river draught of some six feet, but even so she sometimes, in the dry season, stuck fast on a mudbank. A cargo of dark, sweet-smelling bricks of a toffeelike substance called rapadura, made from sugar, were piled on the first deck among sacks of coffee, rice, beans, maté, and bolts of cheap calico. We had a tiny closetlike cabin on the second deck; the afterdeck held a few chairs, a wooden table, and here, too, the passengers slung their hammocks. Two pet monkeys, belonging to one of the passengers, roamed the deck and begged bananas from the cook; all other livestock was on the barge towed a few feet astern in the churning wake of the *Dom Pedro*.

Since leaving Corumbá, I had been so busy unpack-

ing our baggage that I had no time to go on deck.
When I did go out, I was astonished to discover that
although we had covered miles of the winding stream,
the city was still in sight; long after dark we could
see, against the sky, the mellow glow of its electric
lights.

The boat was crowded with cattlemen, hunters, a
Jesuit missionary and a Parecis Indian traveling with
him; most of them had been to Corumbá for supplies. Someone left the boat at nearly every cluster of
huts along the way; the steamer must have stopped
at twenty little landings. We barricaded a small portion of the deck with our baggage and slept on folding cots, as the tiny staterooms were hot and stuffy—
the thermometer read 110 degrees. Matéo insisted on
sleeping on the barge with his huge stallion, Onca.
Frightened at being shut up and enraged at his nearness to the other horses, the stallion had to be put into
a sling and hauled, kicking and squealing, high in the
air, then lowered carefully into the padded stall prepared for him. Long after we were in bed we could
hear Matéo's soothing voice in the darkness, his quiet,
steadying, "So, Boy . . ." and could visualize the huge
hand touching the trembling arched neck as caress-
ingly as a lover touches the satin skin of his mistress.

The first morning I awoke just as the sun lifted its
head above the horizon, to flood with light the water,
the marsh, and the strange tropical trees. All over the

deck were spread the sleeping forms of our fellow
voyagers, a few in hammocks, but most of them
draped carelessly over the bare boards, heads pillowed
on an arm. I pushed aside my mosquito net and tiptoed across to sit on the edge of the Duke's cot.

As far as we could see, over the boundless wastes of
the pantanales—vast marshes dotted with little islands
of pasture lands and groves of trees—the world
seemed truly new, freshly dew-washed. Bend after
bend, loop after loop of the brown stream wound
through lush marsh and tangled swamp, wild and
uninhabited, save by birds and animals and reptiles
that both crawl and climb. Hyacinth macaws, largest
of the parrot family, flew screeching into the swamps
at the boat's approach; sunlight glinted on their daz-
zling blueness. As do others of the parrot family, the
hyacinths often travel in pairs. Later Matéo told me
that if one bird is killed, its mate will stay beside the
body until it, too, dies.

It was chilly, the sun not yet being high enough to
warm the air. A small dugout paddled by two scantily
clad Indians—a man and a woman—shot out from a
small wooden landing; an open palm-thatched hut
stood in the clearing. Smoke from the cooking fire
filtered bluely through the overhanging trees; strange
blossoms, brilliant red and yellow, gave forth exotic
fragrance. The boat slowed, stopped, and the couple
came alongside. The dugout was lashed fast to the
ladder. The carcass of a large red marsh deer, the
cervo, was hauled over the side of the steamer; its

tail was black underneath, instead of white, as in our whitetail deer at home. A small bag of salt, a few bricks of rapadura and a length of bright cloth was handed over in exchange. The dugout glided back to shore, and the paddle wheels churned a foaming swirl as we again forged ahead against the strong current; in the few minutes necessary to take on fresh meat we had drifted nearly a quarter of a mile down stream. Later we passed a small lagoon where a half dozen lontras, big, six-foot, sealike otters, were disporting themselves; these otters are found only in Brazilian rivers. Their protruding eyes and long silky whiskers give them an elderly appearance; one of them looked so much like a church usher, back home, that I was almost homesick. Every time the otters came to the surface they opened their mouths and mewed at the kis-ka-dee flycatchers, which calmly surveyed their gambols from the swinging loops of the tacuaré, the climbing bamboo, that was suspended from tree to tree.

It seemed to me that I was always hungry. By the time the eleven o'clock Brazilian breakfast was served, I felt starved and forgot that I had eaten four rolls with my coffee at eight. These breakfasts were much the same and took a long time to prepare. Meals in camp, I decided, would be à la Américaine, in so far as time and food permitted. The basis was always feijoada, which I had liked so well in Bahia. After you have eaten all you possibly can of it, your plate is heaped with fried, boiled or roast beef, sometimes monkey, sometimes venison, or other game, fish, eggs, and once in a while a vegetable—usually quiabo, a long, green, pointed vegetable fruit which is cooked with meat; it grows on a high bush, and tastes like our tender green peas. A pumpkin with orange-colored flesh and quantities of small green-and-red pepper pods, soaked in vinegar, are also served as vegetables and relishes.

The chickens were always hungry, too. Fearing they lacked greens, and recalling that Dad always put pepper in the hen's laying mash, I asked the Duke if Matéo could go ashore and get them a green pepper. Matéo looked as if he were about to beat his breast and roar. But he went.

Matéo had constituted himself my bodyguard. In the face of his obvious disapproval of me, his solicitous attitude was ludicrous.

After breakfast I squatted on the edge of the barge to watch some cows that were grazing on the pasture along the bank; they had bells fastened to the tips of their horns. Without thinking, I trailed my hand idly in the water and, because it felt so cool, splashed a bit. I heard no sound, but suddenly a hand grasped my belt and jerked me upright so quickly that my feet swung clear of the deck. I gasped in astonishment at Matéo, who held me. "Idiot!" he snapped and walked away.

"What's the idea?" I blazed at the Duke who was running toward me, mopping sweat from his face with a handkerchief. "If you think I'm going to let that big gorilla—"

"Now wait a minute," the Duke interrupted. "Look at this!" Part of a freshly killed steer, being prepared for lunch, was lying near by; the Duke dropped a chunk overboard. Instantly the water was alive with darting fish. That piece of meat was torn into a hundred shreds. It disappeared in half as many seconds. With rabid, ferocious snaps, the wedge-shaped sharklike teeth of these small fish drove through flesh and bone; in their eagerness to get the meat they even bit each other and any member of the school so wounded was almost instantly devoured by his kind. This last has been denied by some scientists, but I saw it happen again and again.

Matéo returned with Mae West in his hands and made as if to drop her overboard. "I, too, show you what happens," he glowered.

"Piranha, cannibal fish," said the Duke, quietly restoring Mae West to safety. "I should have warned you, but I thought of course you knew."

I did know. Long ago I had read everything I could find on the subject. But the river looked so safe—rippling water, wavering shadows where palms leaned to peer at their reflections; the marshes looked so peaceful, cows grazing, and water birds wading in the shallows, it might have been a scene along the Suwannee River in Florida. That is why the tropics are so cruel; in their very beauty, their utter peacefulness, lies their deception and their danger.

Matéo, as though to make amends, dropped on the deck a short, chunky fish with blunt head and gaping massive jaws; the lower one projects considerably. These fish are easily caught with hook and line. The piranhas are all stoutly built, even though they may be eighteen inches or more in length. Evil, coldly malignant eyes stared at us unwinkingly for an instant. Then, with a shrill squeal of rage, it flapped over and over on the bare boards, snapping viciously at a piece of stout copper wire that held the hook; the wire was cut through like a cord. A little sick, I turned away.

A school of piranhas will strip off the flesh, leaving only a skeleton in a few minutes; a wounded person has little or no chance and they often attack human beings or beasts who are merely wading across a shallow stream or pool. Most killers attack prey smaller than themselves, but not the cannibal fish—the larger the game the better they like it! I had an opportunity later to see for myself how dangerous these fish really are. I would rather meet the painted onca, the jaguar, any time.

Now and then we passed little ranches—a house of palm logs, or wattle-and-daub, with steeply pitched roof of thatch, a mango tree, a patch of mandioca, and occasionally a field of maize or yucca fenced with bamboo.

Their inhabitants were chiefly settlers who had emigrated to the region because of the ease of living; with an abundance of game and fish, and wild fruit which could be had for the picking, the acquisition of their daily bread was a simple matter. A quarter of beef usually could be begged from the large fazendas or cattle ranches, or obtained in return for a few hours' work.

The Negro and Indian huts or encampments often looked more prosperous than those of their white neighbors. Plantains were grown, and clumps of guava, orange and banana trees were more numerous. Men and children on the bank stood and watched with envious eyes the small white steamer—their sole connection with the outside world—until it passed from sight and the thin, blue, wood smoke which belched from its funnel merged into the blue haze of the distant mountains. Women were never seen. Woman's place is in the home; they never show themselves to a stranger.

Even my restless spirit could not withstand the soothing quality of the midday heat. With a book, *The Commentaries* of Alvar Nuñez Cabeza de Vaca, famous explorer and one-time governor of Paraguay, I settled myself comfortably in a hammock.

The steamer made slow progress; the load it pulled against the current acted as a drag. A few hours later we tied up to take on firewood near the mouth of the São Lourenco. Two Indians, clad only in a smile, were fishing from a dugout.

The Duke gave them fishhooks in exchange for the use of their boat and we paddled up the narrow, swift brown stream, picking out points of interest as described by Nuñez when he explored the river in the sixteenth century. Horned screamers, steel-gray and large as turkeys, shrieked at us from the topmost branches of strange tropical trees. A grouselike guan croaked gutturally among the bushes; Matéo said that only the male birds utter this peculiar cry. Green parakeets flew in and out of immense communal nests of sticks built in the crotches of large trees; the nests often weigh hundreds of pounds each. Parrots chattered as they swayed back and forth on the lianas or bush ropes that knotted together the dense growth along both shores; vines were spangled with fragrant white and shell-pink blossoms.

"Bet it's a hundred." The Duke mopped the sweat from his face. "Should have brought Matéo to do the paddling." He grinned at the thought.

"Want to sink the boat?" I slapped at the biting, black flies that even in midstream covered my hands and face. Tiny, hard red pimples that itched like Hades were rapidly speckling every inch of the exposed portions of my body.

"Don't scratch like that!" The Duke was worried. "You might get an infection. You must be extremely careful of the tiniest, most inconsequential wound. Why didn't you wear a head net and gloves?"

"Haven't any." I brushed a mosquito from my neck and craned to see a flock of toucans, each looking like something designed after a Picasso nightmare, dart like kingfishers from bank to bank.

"What!" He bit back a fat swearword; I could see

it form upon his lips. "See here! Are you taking your
five grains of quinine every day? And how about your
typhoid shots? You got the full three before you
left?" He had stopped paddling and the dugout,
tossed like a leaf by the current, bumped upon a sand-
spit where huge jacarés, the South American crocodiles, basked on the warm, sun-heated sands; annoyed at our nearness they rolled like water rats into
the stream. They are seldom man-eaters, as are the
African caymans.

"What shots?" I answered the last question first.
"Nobody said anything about any shots. And I don't
like quinine; it's bitter."

The Duke said nothing. We drifted for a few minutes in complete silence.

"That's too bad," he said at last. "But every night
from now on we serve quinine cocktails; and you
drink no water unless it's boiled. Malaria and typhoid
are two things you are *not* going to have, if I can
help it," he finished grimly. We paddled on upstream.
A flock of slim, red-legged waterfowl were wading in
the shallows.

A big red wasp, a dozen stings of which will dis-
able and often kill a strong man, buzzed around my
head. The Duke slapped viciously at it with the paddle. "No net," he growled bitterly. "A nice headache
I brought! Didn't you bring *anything* useful?"

Startled at his tone, peeved at myself for my
stupidity and feeling ill from the bites, I took refuge

in silence. Two big tears traced a channel through the pimples on each side of my nose. I felt miserable.

"Don't cry, darling." He bent toward me solicitously; worried lines creased deep grooves between his brows. "I don't like to play the part of a heavy-handed husband. But you take situations like this too lightly. Suppose you get malaria or typhoid—there won't be a doctor for hundreds of miles. I couldn't bear to have anything happen to you." He fished out a big handkerchief and wiped my tear-streaked face. "You'll be careful in the future?"

I nodded in agreement.

The Duke backed the boat into a tiny cove where the surrounding tree growth thinned. "Because you're a nice girl I'll show you something wonderful. Then we'll have to hurry back; it's almost sundown."

"First lesson," he said gently, starting to part the heavy creepers, many as thick as a man's arm, with the paddle. "Never touch anything in the jungle with your bare hands, unless you've examined it carefully first; it might be a poisonous snake such as the palm viper, or a dangerous vine, or tree." Even as he spoke, the paddle pushed aside a slender, bronze-green vine which immediately became alive; just above us the pseudo-vine writhed like a whiplash through the foliage and a long, narrow head flicked inquiringly about; its luminous eyes gleamed like topaz in the half-light. I dropped flat in the bottom of the boat.

"Thought you liked snakes," chuckled the Duke wickedly.

"I do!" indignantly. "But not so suddenly. Was it a palm viper?"

"No. Liana snake, not poisonous," he explained as he pushed aside the remainder of the matted growth.

At my first close-up of Green Heaven, or Green Hell, depending entirely upon the point of view, my

throat squeezed shut, aching at the poignant beauty of the pantanales. Behind us the river darkened at the approach of night; on the great marshes night falls almost without twilight, the sun sinking down just as it does at sea. Before us lay a sunlit, flooded plain— a plain as it must have been in the beginning, when all the world was young and undefiled by man.

Never have I seen such a wealth of bird life, not even in beautiful Okefenokee Swamp in Georgia, now a wild life refuge. With unlimited food and few human enemies, innumerable creatures on wings great and small, preened, fluttered, cooed, and screamed over the purple pools, the vivid plots of quivering grasses. Birds and water plants were reflected as in a dark-blue mirror.

Splashes of bronze, green, teal-blue, and orange plumage flashed among the marsh growth, where thousands of caeté flags, wild cannas, with their bold, bananalike leaves, towered above the rushes; over the brilliant, odd-shaped blossoms—red, orange, yellow, scarlet—flocks of hummingbirds hovered on pale blurs of wings, their feathers seemed made of emeralds and of sapphires. Flamingoes circled the lagoons on shell-pink velvety wings; screamers cried caru-caru, and flocks of gray ibises added to the din their wailing, two-syllabled notes. Huge armies of ducks flew across the red orb of the sun, that rested its fierce wheel on the dark tip of a palm frond. Magnificent jabiru storks, black heads tilted, crimson collars agleam on snowy bodies, stalked proudly through the lush grass, or posed sedately on one leg in solitary splendor.

From the marsh, from the jungle along the river, the mighty chorus of animal and insect voices, silent through the heat of the day, rose loudly. A red cervo, black tail high, stepped daintily from the rushes, paused, then bent his head and drank. Belated parrots, two by two, flew homeward. I slid my hand into the Duke's.

The glowing ball dropped lower. Masses of feathery clouds—violet, orange, vermillion—floated above the marsh. There were clouds of deepest blue and clouds of carmine edged with cream or flaming gold; there were bars of purple and bands of palest rose. Then the sun sank in a jade green sea and left the darkened marsh, the river, to mourn its death.

Chapter Six

THE FIRST GRASS HUT

Emily Post lays her first egg—We stock up for a long trip—Captain Kidd's Treasure-Trove—Cáceres and its history—Hants—Matto Grosso, Brazil's "Wild West"—Tapir Town—A houseboat on the Paraguay —The Water Mother, another Lorelei—Floating islands—A strange occupant—We hire another engineer—Wild Indians—Matéo and I go hunting—A water lily bridge—Escape from peccaries—Rescue of Matéo—The building of my first grass hut

IT RAINED NEARLY all the way from the São Lourenco to Cáceres. I was glad when we arrived at the interesting old town, built on a plain fifty or more feet above the Rio Paraguay, because it eased a certain tension among the three of us—The Duke, Matéo, and myself.

Ridiculous as it may seem, apparently trivial matters assume great importance when human beings are thrown together closely, day in, day out, on a common venture which serves to separate their interests from the rest of the world. Especially in such heat.

71

I was in disgrace, through no fault of my own. It seemed unfair to blame *me* because Emily Post chose to lay her first egg in Matéo's hat! It was a wretched-looking affair—tattered, torn, with fishhooks stuck around the crown; it looked as though he slept in it, which, as a matter of fact, he did. Emily Post was probably trying to repay him for the pepper. I could not help laughing. The Duke defended Matéo, even though I went out the moment we docked and bought a magnificent ten-gallon sombrero with fringe. Always quiet and self-controlled, my husband was a fine balance wheel, but he was in an embarrassing position. He did not want to criticize me, nor did he wish to offend his indispensable assistant, whose pride he so well knew. Matéo's pride—it was to be his downfall. Although I had extended the olive branch, he stubbornly refused to wear the new sombrero and cleaned up the old one. I couldn't see that a chicken feather or two in the band made any difference—to me it looked the same as always.

"I'll fix you!" I thought.

Meanwhile, all storms, both of nature and man, ceased. The rain stopped, the sun came out, and human relations brightened.

The Duke and Matéo were busy in the markets adding to our supplies. We needed quantities of rice, oatmeal, dehydrated potatoes, condensed milk, evaporated fruits and berries, figs, dates, coffee, tea, salt, chocolate (bitter and sweet), flour, cocoa, dried beans, evaporated soups, and tins of potted meats.

With fish and game plentiful, it seemed extravagant to buy so much, especially at the prices asked in frontier towns—fifty cents for a small tin of potted tongue, for example. But after a few weeks in the interior I discovered that any change in the menu is welcome and that commonplace things, which we in cities take for granted, such as bread or biscuits, are prized above rubies. We had to supply nearly four pounds of food per day for each of the vaqueiros. Native black beans and farinha we bought in large quantities; beef and, once in a while, fresh milk, could be obtained from fazendas along the way. I added a few fripperies of my own to the supplies— peanut butter, canned chicken, and some boxed cheese that would not spoil in the heat and moisture.

My husband, his men, the instruments, most of the baggage, and the supplies left on a launch the day following our arrival at Cáceres; a barge with the pack animals was towed behind it. Matéo and I were to start upriver on a houseboat five days later. He knew the country and the camp site well. Nothing was said about the chickens, but to play safe I sent them ahead with the baggage.

I kept with me the trunk holding grandmother's silver and another large box, much to the Duke's mystification. "Captain Kidd's Treasure-Trove," he called it facetiously. But I knew he was dying of curiosity. Men have such a bump of it.

Although it was early summer and the rivers were in flood, it was the best time for the Duke's reconnaissance of the territory at the foot of the Plan Alto. High water made transportation easier. Many of the streams that empty into the upper Paraguay are not navigable except at this season. The few roads in Matto Grosso were deep in thick red mud; although this same red fertile earth in São Paulo accounts in large part for its great wealth of coffee plantations, I never dreamed that any soil could be so disagreeably adhesive.

I welcomed the few days stay in Cáceres. I wanted to see the country and to learn its history. Dragging the unwilling Matéo along to act as interpreter, I tried to talk with the girls and the women—white or brown—who walked beneath the trees in the praca, or sat in laughing, chattering groups in doorways and peeked shyly from latticed windows. Certainly the women of Cáceres have more liberty than their country cousins, but of opinions regarding matters outside the home, they had none.

Little by little, bit by bit, I wove together the local history of the city and its surroundings. Below lay the great Xarayes Marsh, a vast earthy sponge which absorbs the annual overflow of the upper Paraguay. It was the haunt, so said the townfolk, of tigers, huge snakes, giant crocodiles, and cannibal fish. It was haunted, too, by El Gran Moxo, whose fabled island home was in the heart of the Laguna de los Xarayes. He was the legendary ruler of another El Dorado; at night the lights in his palace still burned. Early explorers believed this legendary lake to be the source of the Paraguay; the marsh in the rainy season is about three hundred miles long and almost a third as wide. The Paraguay, main tributary of the Rio Parana, actually has its origin in seven lagoons in the heart of the Pari Mountains of Matto Grosso; it flows through Xarayes, separates Bolivia from Matto Grosso, and Paraguay from the Argentine. The few settlers who live in Xarayes either must grow fins, or depend on dugouts for their transportation.

When they learned that my destination was innermost Matto Grosso, the staid folk of Cáceres looked at me pityingly, indulgently, sorrowfully—but all agreed that I was a little mad. "Muy lejos—off the earth," they said, tapping their foreheads significantly. But they treated me most respectfully—from a safe distance—for people of the hinterlands revere those who are a little touched. Innocentes, they call them. After listening to a few tales of Indian proficiency with poisoned arrows, outlaws, dead bodies found floating down the flooded river, and danger from tigers, man-eating snakes, and women-crazed crocodiles (the meat is more tender, Senhora), I agreed with them.

Matto Grosso, the great wilderness, is the most romantic and, in theory, the most lawless of the Brazilian provinces. Gossip claims it is a land of stinking swamps, of sun-baked cattle plains, of wooded hills, and countless streams. Gossip says it is peopled with hot-tempered, dark-skinned Brazilians, who are proud of their Portuguese ancestry; some of them, like the Paulistas, are of mixed Indian and Portuguese blood; there are a few Negroes whose ancestors were brought in chains from Africa—today they are gaily clad, silver-spurred gauchos; Serbians, who trek from ranch to ranch, their mules laden with packs of dry goods and household appliances; Japanese coffee growers, who keep to themselves and save their hard-earned money that they may return with fortunes to their native land. It is rumored that these people are unduly suspicious of strangers and bow to no law but that of the Smith & Wesson slung at their hips.

Gossip is right. Matto Grosso and its people are all of these things, and more. But gossip neglects to state that these same settlers and ranch hands also are kind, generous, and trustworthy, once they accept you as a friend; with the exception of their womenfolk, who live in haremlike seclusion (in the kitchen), all that they own is yours. Of our crew of fourteen, only one man proved worthless. He was a ferret-faced, bitter, pathetic American who had failed as a rancher in Entre Rios; the remaining men, except Matéo, were all Brazilians.

On fine sunny days Matéo and I explored the low, rolling hills of the heavily forested countryside. Serra Azull, the Blue Ridge, extends from Cáceres to Cuyabá, capital of Matto Grosso. From this city Colonel Fawcett, in 1925, with two companions—one of them his son—set out in search of a lost world, the

mythical home of the last Incas. None of the party
was ever seen again.

Matéo rode his black Onca and I tried out the
cream-colored colt the Duke gave me for a present.
It was a beauty, with flowing black tail and crinkly
mane, named Tiger; its name suited it to a T. With
bared teeth he charged anything human that walked
—people on horseback were quite safe. He fought
every second until he was bridled and saddled, but
once mounted, no rider could ask for a better, more
docile horse—fast, smooth-gaited, and sure-footed.
This last is most important—the trails are slippery as
a greased pig. I was crazy about Tiger, but Matéo
hated him. Once, in an unguarded moment, the colt
borrowed a small piece from the seat of the gaucho's
pants. It was unfortunate that they fitted so tightly.

It rained again the day Matéo and I started for
Tapirapoan, our last contact with civilization. The
village, Tapir Town on the River of Tapirs (I saw
none of these mammals until after we reached camp),
was small, with a ranch at the head of navigation on
the Rio Sepotuba. I was so excited at leaving for the
real wilderness that I scarcely noticed the downpour
of icy water that dropped from the black sky. Gusts
of wind and spray swept through every crack and
crevice of the hide-covered toldo, the house built on
the deck of the native prancha which we had rented.
Pranchas are scowlike houseboats that drift down the

rivers, stopping wherever they choose, and are poled upstream or given a tow by some passing launch or steamer. These houseboats are often the only stores ranchers in the interior see for years; they carry the simple necessities of life and give the settlers a bonus by way of a bit of gossip or news of the world outside.

The sturdy little launch which towed us upstream chugged briskly away in the very center of the river, pulling its heavy load without faltering; our launch and houseboat were a tandem, not a team, as channels of swift streams are tricky. Despite the high water, which on stretches of the river may rise thirty feet or more, we passed two small boats stranded on sand bars.

Nine of us were crowded in the windowless cabin: Matéo, the vaqueiros—Cauto and Julio—the Portuguese owner and his family of four, and myself. The horses and pack mules were tethered on the open deck in back of the toldo.

Our cook, wife of the owner, was a full-blooded Guaraní (so she said). Certainly she had the clear-cut features and swaying, effortless walk of that ancient race; she moved like a dancer on flat, bare feet, swinging her hips. I wondered if she went to sleep with the short black cigar which always seemed stuck in her mouth; oddly enough, I never saw her asleep. Even with three babies clinging to her full skirts, she did all of her work and most of the Senhor's too.

The Senhor was a small, faded wisp of a man, with

sad bovine eyes and drooping mustache. He was a picturesque figure, dressed in what I thought was the
native chiripa, the breechclout, but a second glance
disclosed the fact that he merely had pulled the tail
of his gaudy checked shirt between his legs and
tucked it under the front of the broad leather belt
he wore about his middle. On great occasions, when
we stopped at ranches along the river, he wore over
this outfit a stylish soft fringed apron of tanned
deerskin. His puitan, a brilliant scarlet blanket, slit-
ted in the center like a poncho, he used only in clear
weather. "Rain no hurt skin, hurt puitan," said he.

Late that evening the rain cleared and Matéo made
a nest of blankets for me in the bow of the boat. Snug
under my mosquito net, I cuddled down in comfort;
the night was cool, with a strong wind sweeping up
from the south. It took me a long time to accept the
fact that below the equator cool breezes blow from
the south, and that the north side of a house is the
sunny side.

Stars pricked out, one by one, in a pale-gray sky.
The heavens became studded with faint twinkling
lights; they seemed but pale reflections of the torches
carried by millions of fireflies whirling in a frenzied
dance above the narrow strips of marsh paralleling
the river. There was no moon. The forest beyond the
plains loomed black and forbidding. Shadowy night
birds swept like phantoms across the surface of the
water; eerie cries drifted back on the breeze. Occa-

sionally a fish leaped and jacarés surged among the
reeds along the shore.

I felt very close to the hidden mysteries of nature.
For the first time I understood something of the
inner force which causes men, whose lives have been
passed chiefly in the open, to prefer death in the
jungle to life in the city. I closed my eyes tightly
and strove for close communication with nocturnal
wilderness ways. In the pulsing darkness I could hear
the silken swish of palm fronds on the shore and the
lapping of waves against the boat. Suddenly, a Lorelei
of the forest burst into a strain of melody so sweet,
so clear, so poignant, that I held my breath in order
not to miss even the faintest liquid note. "Mae d'agua
—the Water Mother," Matéo whispered reverently.
Although I knew it was the song of an unseen bird,
I accepted his superstition as natural, a part of the
night. In Cáceres I had heard the legend of the Water
Mother—a woman with face and form of surpassing
beauty—another Lorelei with golden hair and golden
voice, who lures men to their drowning. Unlike the
legendary mermaid, the Mae d'agua is not half fish.
She has legs and no tail. There are dozens of stories
about the Water Mother. Children love her.

The boat eased slowly around a bend; it picked
up speed as we straightened out again in the channel.
Instinctively my eyes followed the light path in the
center of the river and focused on a large dark patch
about ten feet in diameter. It was headed directly
toward us. "Camelotte, floating island," Matéo ex-

plained. I often had seen small ones drifting down the
stream, but never one so large. I moved to the side
of the boat to get a closer view and Matéo obligingly
held the large flash; sometimes these bits of sedge,
pampas grass, and reeds are inhabited by strange cast-

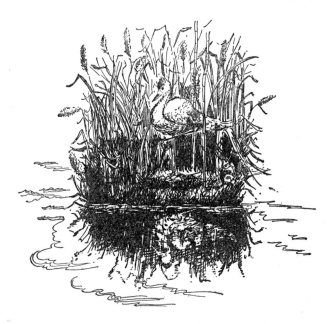

aways—snakes, crocodiles, monkeys, or other reptiles
or beasts caught when the islands crumble away from
the bank. The Senhora stood, feet braced, with boat
hook and pole poised, ready to ward off the island
should it come too near. The Senhor danced excitedly
up and down. "Catch it! Catch it!" he shrieked,
meaning the opposite. An especially large and ferocious mosquito breeds on these islets and rivermen

avoid them as they would the plague. Egged on by
her husband, and herself excited, the Senhora leaned
far over and gave a vicious poke to a dark mass centered in a nest of grass. Like a coiled spring the mass
erupted, snatched the pole from the startled woman,
dropped the hook over the rail, and the tallest,
thinnest man I have ever seen vaulted lightly to the
deck of the houseboat. His strange raft, released from
the hook, swirled merrily down the current, narrowly
missed disaster at the bend, and disappeared from
sight. The extraordinary castaway brought with him
the entire mosquito population of Matto Grosso, or
so it seemed. Their shrill drones almost drowned out
the fervid prayers of the Senhor, who actually believed the visitor to be from another world.

Amazed, amused, I listened to Matéo's questioning.
His name? "Senhor Candido Mariana da Silva Rondon Vargas, may it please the Senhora . . ." address-
ing his remarks to me in fluent Spanish, of which I
understood about every tenth word. Matéo translated. "After the great General Rondon who explored
and mapped the Matto Grosso and made the country
safe for settlers, did he not make friends and control
the wild Indians of the interior? Did he not guide
down the Rio Teodoro the former President of a
great country—Estados Unidos—and did he not keep
El Presidente Teodoro Roosevelt safe? Is not the General the greatest man in all Brazil? And who should
know better than I, personalmente? The greatest engineer who ever focused the cross hairs of a transit!"

"You are an engineer?" queried Matéo skeptically. But yes, he was—a deluge of affirmation almost drowned us; he had worked in Uruguay, in Paraguay, and now roved through the wilderness from ranch to ranch and town to town, surveying, according to his tale, more land than the country could boast. He was also a water witch, finding—with a forked stick —water where no water had ever been before.

"You are well-named, Dom Candido," remarked Matéo. "Well, we will see; you are hired." We really needed an extra man, as Matéo's services were largely diverted to watching me. That is, during good weather, when I was on the move.

During bad weather Matéo spent most of his time talking to the pilot, or plaiting a new lasso of fine tanned leather thongs. The vaqueiros ate and slept; never have I seen people more versed in both arts. The first day I was amused, the second I was annoyed, and the third I was downright angry. That was the day we met the missionary.

We were making good time up the Sepotuba. Dom Candido and I were standing at the door of the toldo, watching the slanting lines of rain dashing into the flowing road, when a batalão, a thirty-foot boat built of planks over stout wooden ribs, spun around a sharp bend, struck a projecting tree root, and ran into the bank. An arched, palm-thatched shelter covered the center of the craft. Beneath the thatch roof sat two men, one gaunt and yellowed by fever, the other bright-eyed and alert. Neither man moved to

help the Indian paddlers, four in number, down whose
bronze nude bodies the water ran in tiny rivulets.
After they had repaired the boat, they replaced their
bright calico loin cloths. We moored near by.

Dom Candido laughed at my excitement. I thought
how like a fang his sole remaining tooth appeared, as
he threw back his head and howled with glee. But
these were the first real wild Indians I had ever seen!

Matéo moved quickly to the rail and called to
the man, asking if they needed assistance. The gaunt
one, a trader, replied in the negative. With his com-
panion, a missionary, he was carrying a load of skins
—snake, jaguar, ocelot, puma—to Cáceres; he bar-
tered, also, to the ranchers along the rivers, bright
colored pottery, an occasional bracelet of tigers' teeth,
Brazil nuts, and Indian featherwork and arrows from
the Amazon valley. I never discovered why settlers
in Matto Grosso collect the last two items.

"Ask him about the Indians," I entreated Matéo,
but he turned indifferently away. "Paren-tin-tins,"
interposed Dom Candido. "Saw them when I worked
at Monte Cristo, a rubber station on the Guaporé.
Many persons come from the Madeira to trade in
Cáceres and Corumbá." Matéo glared at him; he was
forced to interpret, but already a feud had arisen
between them.

Paren-tin-tins! Chunky bodies smeared with blue
paint in grotesque zigzag lines and circles; straight
hair cut in a Dutch bob; one had hair that showed a
reddish tinge, the others black, thick and tangled.

I watched the batalão until gray lines of rain hid it from my view. The Duke had told me yarns aplenty about these little people, the wildest, fiercest of the Amazon tribes that harassed the engineers, particularly surveying parties far from camp, who built the Madeira-Mamoré railroad.

Cannibalistic tendencies are attributed to the Paren-tin-tins, but what interested me most about them was the fact that they apparently have developed a physical protection against the dreaded candiru, a minute fish, almost microscopic, which attacks bathers by working its way through the urethra; only an operation can remove the fish from the duct leading to the bladder. This fish is the most peculiar and painful of all the pests inhabiting the streams of the Amazon jungles. Its name—candiru (penis fish)— signifies its menace. For centuries the Paren-tin-tins, and perhaps other tribes, have so closely bound the foreskin of their male babies, pulling it out and folding it over, that Nature has developed a greatly lengthened protective covering. A rolled leaf or bark guard is sometimes worn for additional safety.

There were now ten of us shut up together on one houseboat and we began to get on each others nerves. The boat moved so slowly, scarcely a mile an hour, that by the end of the sixth day I felt like screaming at the men to hurry up and get to Tapira-poan; we had at least twenty more hours to spend on board.

I played a bit with the babies, cute little chaps dressed only in pink or blue shirts reaching to the belly button in their fat brown tummies. One of them drank my shampoo and I suffered agonies, expecting him to die; nothing happened, he wasn't even sick.

The seventh day the sun came out. Matéo checked our supplies, then decided to go hunting; fresh meat would break the monotony of our bread and beans diet. I persuaded him to let me tag along and see the sights.

We left the boat and followed a little path, hard trodden by the queer splayed feet of capybaras, huge piglike rodents as large as a half-grown sheep. Along the river we had seen them sitting on their haunches in the water, with only their blunt, short-eared heads above the surface; their meat is very tender, tasting like rabbit.

The game trail ran close to the river's edge, but we seldom saw the stream; long trailing branches, tied together by thousands of curling, looping vines, dropped to the water and formed a matted green curtain so dense that only occasionally did we glimpse the opposite shore. Matéo moved swiftly but silently on tough bare feet; I slid after him as best I could, my best being as silent as an elephant herd making for water. Twice he hissed at me and then, seeing I was having a bad time with my heavy field boots, slashed a lane through the thorny scrub and entered the jungle beyond. Here the walking was easier.

Shafts of light broke through the foliage of the tall trees; slim saplings pushed their heads toward the sun; canes, bamboo, and reeds grew thickly in damp spots. I felt as though I were in a magnificent greenhouse and the intense, humid heat increased this feeling. My flannel shirt was soaked with perspiration and tiny drops rolled down my face like tears, but Matéo never turned a hair.

We came to a tiny clearing in the jungle. I stood still, completely enchanted. Brazil is a land of trees; so many kinds—there were trees with yellowed trunks, low trees with long thick leaves, tall trees with foliage as delicate as Paraguayan lace, trees with thick swollen boles straddling pools of black water, trees with stiff black thorns. Great clumps of orchids, and bromelias—they belong to the pineapple family— clung to trunks and perched aloft on branches, their blossoms—white, yellow, lilac, purple—vivid against the less showy greens. Morning glories in white and blue and rose trailed over stumps and clambered up unresisting fig trees. The bamboos had fine feathery foliage; the palms, "wawasa"—buriti—those that the natives call the Tree of Life, I liked best of all. From the palms they secure food, shelter, and fuel. While I stood gazing admiringly at them, some with leaves as fine as that of the bamboo growing beside them and others with thirty foot fronds, Matéo, a few paces distant, to my astonishment suddenly began to recite in English:

"Mine is the country where the palm trees rear
   Their stately heads toward the azure sky,
And where in accents soft and clear,
   The sabia sings her hymn of melody;
Here, in my exile, say what warblers rare
Can with the sabia's notes their own compare?"

I listened with a new respect for the rough, often uncouth, harsh gaucho. Never had I suspected this side of his nature. I was to learn there is a deep poetic strain in those of Guaraní blood. Was this Matéo? I did not interrupt . . .

"Our life's a dream of love in fairy bowers,
   Where nature's lavish gifts are ever rife;
Bright land of palms, where sweet the sabia sings,
The exile's heart to thee still fondly clings."

He turned abruptly and plunged into the jungle. I hurried to catch up with him. "It was beautiful," I said sincerely. "Will you write me a copy in English, so I may learn it, too?" He did not answer. Rebuffed, I dropped behind. Months later I traced the poem, "Cançao do Exilio," Song of the Exile. Its author, A. Gonçalves Dias, a homesick exile, was drowned when returning to the Brazil he loved so well.

It seemed to me I had walked for hours and nothing had happened—no adventures such as fill the pages of modern thrillers—no wild Indians, no tigers, no snakes, although I knew that Matéo's keen eyes had scanned carefully every foot of trail, above and

below. I am not afraid of snakes—not much, anyway—and the packet of serum in Matéo's pocket
made me bold and venturesome. "Bring on your
death-dealing reptiles, your horrors!" I mentally
taunted the gods that be. "I can find more dangers
in New York's city streets."

The jungle thinned. In a moment we stood upon
the bank of a long, narrow lagoon. Matéo growled
in disgust; no capybaras squatted in its tannin-colored
waters. But on the surface of the poisonously beautiful pool was something that I appreciated more—
atolls of emerald green, smooth, six foot in diameter,
circles of *Victoria regia* leaves in their natural home,
each one encircled by an upturned crimson rim,
ringed by sharp spines. A fallen tree trunk leaned
far across the pool. I walked out on it, carefully,
under Matéo's watchful eye, to examine at close hand
the thick, rubbery leaves of the lilies; a string of
tiny fish bats, disturbed by the shaking of the tree,
abandoned their siesta and flew in a long file across
the water.

I had always heard that these lily leaves would
bear the weight of a man; if so, surely they would
hold my hundred pounds—ninety-seven now, for the
heat had melted away still more of me. I glanced at
Matéo. He was walking slowly along the bank, head
tipped back, scanning the trees at the edge of the
lagoon. I knew he was looking for marecas, rosy-bill
ducks that often sit in long rows on tree limbs. These
ducks give a whistling call similar to that of the

widgeon, which they resemble; they have bright pink
bills.

Cautiously I placed one foot squarely in the center
of a large pad and pushed hard; the leaf was scarcely
indented. Emboldened, I dropped lightly from the
tree trunk, teetered a moment, and balanced myself
by extending my arms like a tightrope walker; my
little raft slid beneath me like a rug on a waxed floor.
The heavy ropelike stem which anchored it still allowed it plenty of room to shift about; already my
tree trunk was out of reach. While I hesitated, uncertain as to the depth of the pool—I can't swim—

"Come back from there," shouted Matéo angrily.

My leaf skidded and I sprang to the next pad, like
Eliza crossing the ice.

"What you theenk? You theenk you're a Jesus
Christ bird?" he bellowed with no thought of irrev-
erence. Jacana, the bird so-named by the natives because it appears to walk or skate serenely over the
water, has glossy-brown body plumage shading into
violet at its throat; a vivid red fold of skin lies at
the root of its bill. These birds are generally on the
move; above Matéo's howls of rage I could hear the
ringing zip, zip, zip of their cries as they sped across
the aquatic growth on long, slender, clawed toes.

I was surprised and delighted to find that the thick
matted pads would actually hold me up. I was even
more pleased at the idea of luring Matéo onto a leaf,
feeling quite sure that although I could cross the pool
by a lily-pad bridge, he could not. The other shore,

fringed with palms and bamboo, looked mysterious and inviting, so I just kept on going, teetering from one leafy steppingstone to another; if I failed to step squarely in the center, or chose too small a pad, disaster—sooner or later—was inevitable, but I heedlessly refused to consider this and shouted to Matéo to come on.

But Matéo, yelling with rage and fright behind me, had seen something that I did not see. He had seen flat-sided shapes slipping like gray shadows between the jointed bronze-green stems of the bamboos—a drove of the deadliest cloven-footed beasts that run in packs—the white-lipped peccaries, hunting not only roots and grubs but anything which they could fall upon and rend to pieces with their knifelike tusks. Matéo shouted himself hoarse, but I was so interested I did not notice what he said and kept on, glancing over my shoulder to see if he was following.

He was. With no alternative he sprang, lightly for so huge a man, onto a spot where pads, stems, and broken tree branches were thickest. By sheer strength, he lunged ahead five or six feet before they sank beneath him like a sinking ship. The more he struggled to get out of the waist-deep mud and water, the deeper he sank. I could not help laughing, not only because he looked funny, but because he was so mad. I certainly was even with Matéo! It did not occur to me that he might have difficulty getting out.

But suddenly some sixth sense warned me of danger.

Before Matéo's immediate and ominous quiet, his swollen face, almost purple from exertion, I stood silent. It was then I heard the strange moaning grunts behind me. I whirled, slipped, regained my balance, and saw the shore lined with lean, bristly peccaries, a huge herd of thirty or more; evil white lips drawn back in a snarl from blood-reddened tusks, they literally foamed at the mouth as they hesitated on the brink of the treacherous pool. A few feet of clear water was between them, the lily pads, and me.

I retreated faster than I had advanced. Almost to safety, I glanced back at Matéo. He had sunk nearly to his armpits. In a panic I turned and stepping cautiously, went as close to him as I dared. Muck or quicksand, we both knew without words there was no time to go for aid, even if I could have found the way back, which I could not do. In that instant my childish resentment of Matéo's attitude vanished. What had I done! There was no reproach in his eyes, but he was sinking visibly, inch by inch, though he no longer moved a muscle. I remembered a cow caught in a boghole at home—her eyes, her patient acceptance . . .

"Get a big vine," he said quietly. "Swing it over here. Don't fall in."

I hurried to the shore, such a few feet to safety, and seized a great festooned liana. It was twisted and twined so tightly to the trees I could not budge it. I tore and pulled, wept and complained, cursed and cried out in fear. I dared not look back. My hands were cut and bleeding, my nails torn to the quick, but I could not loosen the vine. In despair I abandoned it, looked helplessly about, then saw, almost beside me, a doubled, twisted rope vine swinging free. How had I missed seeing it? . . . In thirty seconds it was in Matéo's hands.

No one but a man of Matéo's strength could have pulled himself from that mire. Great muscles swelling, inch by inch, he began to work his way out. I pushed broken branches into the shallows and dragged fallen bamboos over them; flat on my stomach I inched out until I could push two stout poles beneath his armpits. When the suction lessened, he looped the vine securely around him, then with its aid crawled slowly and painfully, flat on his stomach, over the pads, the poles distributing his weight. After what seemed hours, but was in reality only minutes, he reached the shore. Spines from the pads were imbedded deeply in his hands and legs.

Destitute of life, the palm-thatched, mud-built huts—now inhabited only by bats and owls—sprawled upon a little hill. Uncharted jungle crept to its very foot. All that remained of a man's hopes and dreams lay before me, a scant patch of mandioca, a neglected orange grove, a few wild plantains. Fences were destroyed and game had rooted up the crops.

As I halted on the knoll, jungle fowl fled into the bush and flocks of green parrakeets flew shrieking from the fields. This was our camp site. Here would be my first home.

It was nearly dark. Sunset embers stained the west dull copper.

The camp looked deserted. A sliver of bare land ran from the brow of the hill a hundred feet into the forest. Tiger quickened his pace at the sight of horses, mules, and pack oxen tethered at one end of the clearing. A waterproof tent showed light against the dark trees beyond; a fire burned brightly before it. I looked in vain for the newly built house which I had expected.

In the distance I heard Matéo shouting at the pack animals. Dom Candido, mounted on a gaunt gray jenny mule, was riding swiftly down the trail; in the gathering darkness the path looked like a gay red ribbon dropped by a careless hand. I dismounted and dropped Tiger's reins on the ground; impatient as he was to be with the other horses, he was well-trained and would stand thus for hours.

I fastened back the tent flap and stepped inside. It was cool and quiet—but empty of life. I had known it would be. Had the Duke been in camp he would have been watching for us; also, the tent would not have been left unguarded. What had happened? Where were the vaqueiros? And where was my home? The grass hut I had been led to expect, to which I

Upper: Most Indian villages are built close to small streams; these last provide not only drinking water and bathing facilities, but furnish stones for
laundry work as well. *Lower:* Cable railway from Santos to São Paulo. Most
of the world's supply of coffee is carted over this road.

Left: Many small boats used on South American rivers are designed like those for use on shallow streams in North America. Poling is commonly practiced on inland rivers. *Right:* Bows and arrows are still important to Brazilian Indians; this family has just returned from a fishing expedition. The natives are very adept at this type of fishing.

had looked forward with such hopes, such longing, did not exist.

Discouraged, tired, and scared, I sat down upon one of the camp chairs and looked about. The tent was small and cluttered. Our cots, gay covers awry, were placed against the wall; mosquito netting hung like canopies above them; books and instruments were strewn upon the folding table standing on the canvas floor. A transit, a level, and other tools were piled carefully upon the metal cases in which were packed our clothing and our food.

Matéo entered. Two men staggered behind him, lugging my trunk and my precious box. Replying to my eager questions, he said the men were camped at the foot of the hill. Orders of the Senhor Boss. I breathed a sigh of relief; we would have the hilltop to ourselves. My husband? He was working, of course, what did I expect? He would be back in a couple of days. The hut? Oh, that would be built tomorrow; the Duke had left ten men for that purpose.

Confused, uncertain, I picked at the boiled beef and beans Matéo served me. Then, without undressing, I curled up on one of the cots. My head ached. I had felt unlike myself ever since we left Tapirapoan. Once beyond the village, with its friendly inhabitants, we had ridden due north for a few miles, along the right-of-way of the Brazilian Telegraphic Commission which, headed by General Rondon, had explored and opened communication from Matto Grosso's capital, Cuyabá, to Porto Velho on the Madeira. We then turned northwest through virgin territory, following the trail left by the Duke's crew as they cut a passage for the heavy wooden-wheeled baggage carts. The heat at midday was intense, although we were now about a thousand feet above sea level.

Somber walls of dense tropical forest lined the wide swath and in places already was encroaching on the trail; even well-built roads, in jungle country, unless constantly cared for, in a few months are completely engulfed by lush new growth. False bellbirds, gray instead of white like the true bellbird, flitted through the tops of the trees; black howlers roared from the thickets.

My first night in camp I slept badly. Once I awoke and saw Matéo's huge bulk stretched before the opened tent flap, bare feet outthrust to the fire; his head was covered tightly with a heavy blanket. Thoughts of vampire bats ran through my mind. The jenny mule had been attacked on the way to camp and had suffered greatly from loss of blood; she was not yet fully recovered. I went to sleep again and dreamed of hordes of bats who left huge tracks in the sandy soil, all of them turned backwards as related in an old Guaraní tale, so they could be easily recognized.

Sun shining in my face awakened me; already it was climbing up the sky.

Matéo looked in, smiling smugly at seeing me at last safely delivered to camp, and observing that I was awake, brought me a cup of coffee, hot, pungent,

brewed from freshly roasted and ground beans. My
headache was gone. I was anxious to be up and about;
there were boxes to unpack, a house to put to rights—
when it was built.

When it was built, did I say!

Like an Aladdin's palace the basketlike palm framework, the skeleton of my first hut, already stood on

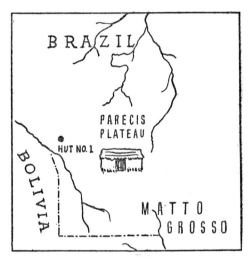

the hilltop. It looked enormous, too large for two
people. I stood appalled before it.

Two huts, ten feet by fourteen each, were joined
together by a six-foot, roofed-in space between. Doors
opened into this corridor. Here we could sling our
hammocks on sultry nights. Mosquito netting, not
such as we use in the States but a finely woven cloth,
covered the exposed sides; it was weighted by heavy
wooden poles at the bottom. Each hut had a large

glassless window, one to the south, one to the north, also covered with mosquito bar; when the bamboo shutters and doors were opened wide, all the breezes of the plains swept through.

The vaqueiros, copper, brown, dusky black—most of them were caboclos, half-breeds—with a preponderance of Indian blood, were grabbing huge fistfuls of gluey mud from a near-by puddle and squeezing it between the sticks. Dom Candido, hands on hips, strutted like a rooster as he superintended the job.

That reminded me that I had neither seen nor heard the chickens. Matéo said they were fastened in one of the old ranch houses, until a proper coop could be built.

The very air quivered. It was 104 degrees in the shade. Distant and remote, the sky seemed filled with tiny dancing stars whenever I raised my eyes. Strange, new types of palms, rearing their heads above the orange and scarlet blossoms of wild plantains, cast no shadows. Long-tailed trogans, red-and-green plumage aglitter, whistled their loud, thrice-repeated call from the cashew thicket behind the south hut.

Matéo slung my hammock in the shade of a ceiba. I swung idly back and forth, watching blue and yellow lizards scamper over the new thatch of the huts; their feet made faint rustlings among the stiff, bronze-green palm leaves.

I awoke at sundown. My home was finished. Matéo, Dom Candido, the vaqueiros, all had disappeared;

their voices, their songs, came to me on the evening breeze.

I thought, with a feeling of wonder, how far away I now was from home; more than five thousand miles from New York, at least twelve hundred miles northwest of Rio de Janeiro, but, like any young bride, I was anxious to get settled in my new home. I could scarcely wait to move in. Yet I was all alone on the hilltop.

Chapter Seven

HOME IN THE WILDERNESS

*A table set for two—Green orchids—My first home
—A jungle murder—Jungle concert—Grandmother's
clock—The Duke had not come home—Dom Poco-
mas—Hunting by a jungle lagoon—The wailing
frog—Brigham disappears*

RAIN PATTERED CEASELESSLY on the new thatch of
my first home. It sifted in a fine spray through the
palm-leaf roof and spread in dark patches on the
freshly whitewashed walls. It misted with minute
drops the waterproof silk canopy stretched above the
linen-covered table set for two. Light from the Juno
oil lamp shone dimly on thin silver, worn down by
firm New England hands, and on thick pottery—the
color of clotted cream, shaped by clay-daubed Indian
fingers. Heat, heavy and smothering, was spread like
a blanket over the room. Only the pale-green orchids,
lettuce-crisp in a crimson bowl, were untouched by
its withering blast.

Beyond the window the land lay dark and silent;

the tiny pool of light beneath reached no farther than the overhanging eaves. The vaqueiros, in their leafy shelters, were silent, too. Dom Candido's braggart tones did not reach me on the hilltop, and even Matéo's boisterous voice was stilled. The cooking fires long since had burned to embers; there were no songs of love, no songs of deeds of valor.

The Duke had not come home.

I awoke that morning at cockcrow. The reek of wet sod mingled with the fragrance of a thousand flowers; borne on the morning breeze, the scent drifted through the open tent flap. I walked over to the huts, unhooked the mosquito cloth, and went in. The house stood on the very brink of the hill, which dropped steeply to the hollow. Through the open window of the north hut I could see far into the dark masses of the forest, which crept almost within reach; tree trunks were green with moss, and orchids and bromelias clothed the branches with red and purple; bamboos and lianas, decked with blossoms, grew at the wood's edge. The south window framed open country, rolling hills dotted with clumps of trees. It might have been a New York pasture, except that, instead of cattle, three red deer browsed on the lush grass and sheltered in the thickets. The cervos never had been hunted, so they were not afraid.

We worked hard all that morning, whitewashing the inside of the huts, moving boxes, setting up cots, and placing folding chairs and tables. The Duke was expected by noon and I wanted everything finished by then, to surprise him.

At eleven we began to listen for the first faint sound of the shrill drone which would announce his coming—the loud creaking noise which by its very monotony would seem almost a part of Matto Grasso, like the repetitious chirp of swallows on a late summer's night. This sound soon becomes familiar in the hinterlands, where huge hide-covered carts, drawn by four to six oxen, drag slowly along lonely roads; the noise of solid-wood wheels which turn, axle and all, beneath the wagon body.

The men ate their eleven o'clock breakfast as they worked. By twelve the house was ready. We sat around talking, laughing, waiting for the first whining note from the baggage cart. One hour, two, three, four . . . no sign of the Duke. "Is there nothing we can do?" I begged Matéo. He shook his head.

We were in nearly virgin country. To the north dwelt stark-naked tribes, great fighting tribes, who raided native villages and carried off the women; near by were the peaceful Parecis Indians of the plateau, who played a game resembling football with their heads—they bunted the ball off the ground with great dexterity and speed. Less than one hundred and fifty miles to the west was Bolivia; to the southeast was the Rio Sepotuba and the fringe of civilization. To the south was sparsely settled country. Where were we to look?

A cold drizzling rain began. At the foot of the

hill the vaqueiros had built palm-thatched shelters beneath which they crouched around small fires. Matéo issued quantities of maté or Paraguayan tea, and the gourd—filled with the steaming hot brew of the holly leaves—passed from hand to hand; the bombilla, or tube through which it is sipped, passed from mouth to mouth. To refuse to drink in this manner is an unforgivable insult to one's host.

Five o'clock, six, seven . . . the men were restless. Matéo and Dom Candido talked together in low tones. I demanded to know what was wrong.

Cauto, one of the cooks, for some obscure reason of his own, told his companions we were camped on the very spot where a man was murdered—the former ranch owner, I judged. His spirit, Cauto said, attacked and killed all so bold as to trespass on his property; he, Cauto, had seen him sitting with them around the camp fires. Proof? Had the Senhor Boss returned? This was proof enough for the superstitious vaqueiros. Even Matéo was uneasy. Only the dark and dangerous trail prevented the men from deserting in a body. They would leave at dawn, they said, unless the Duke returned unharmed tonight. According to us stranded in the wilderness; self-preservation was their code there was nothing dishonorable in leaving every man's right.

Matéo unlocked the metal cases in which the food was kept and passed out a pint of native rum to each. Recklessly he broke into the store delicacies: white sugar, condensed milk—a thick gooey mass which they ate from the end of a stick dipped into the cans, sweet chocolate, and tins of biscuits. Julio, the other cook, already had prepared thick venison steaks and choice cuts of tapir meat for broiling; a dozen black muscovies, which the natives call patos, were plucked and drawn ready to roast on grids before the flames. I never became accustomed to the amount of food consumed by men living in the open.

We carried the portable phonograph down to the camp and soon "Love's Old Sweet Song," the Duke's favorite, was floating out into the jungle night. They clustered around the phonograph like children, their fears almost forgotten. The liquor loosened their tongues and gave them false courage; even Cauto, the troublemaker, became brave and affable. They loved "O Susanna" and the Victor Herbert songs, but they had only scant applause for jazz. Wild, dark faces smiled at me; they shouted, sang with the music, although they could not understand a word of English, and improvised dances which suited the mood of the moment.

Superstitious fears did not affect their appetites. I could not eat. An iron band seemed welded around my throat. Even Matéo only toyed with his food, he who ate two ducks at a meal and bellowed for more.

Nine o'clock! I put on the last record. Above the drip, drip of the rain, Wagner's thunderous creation, "Ride of the Valkyries"—his portrayal of the triumphant dash of Wotan's daughters carrying the souls of the slain to Valhalla—poured forth. The vaqueiros

listened with delight. "Again," they begged. "Again."
Over and over I played the record, until Matéo or-
dered the men to their hammocks for the night.
They went, but I doubt if they slept.

Matéo's powerful flashlight threw a broad beam
before us. We climbed the hill in silence. The light
picked out the huts around which wild vines already
twined and twisted as though no hand had touched
them. Under the gaucho's watchful eye hundreds of
plants in full bloom had been lifted before sunup
from their homes and moved to mine. Their vitality
was so great, their growth so luxuriant, that life-
giving sap continued to flow without a check through
their stems and veins. In one day new tendrils had
put forth to cling to the new home.

Inside the house the air felt chill and damp. Matéo
lighted the lamps. I wandered about, doing all the
unnecessary things women do while waiting. I
changed my clothes, just to have something to do.
The south hut, our bedroom, looked inviting with its
cool, clean, bare white walls. The floor was hard-
trodden earth. One of the metal food cases made my
dressing table, the other held personal effects of my
husband. Our cots were covered with gay blue and
white spreads; their legs stood in small tins partially
filled with kerosene; without this insect precaution,
the beds would crawl with pests. A shower bath
would be wonderful, I mused, as I poured water
from a kerosene tin over my hands. Tomorrow I'll

talk to the Duke about it. I shut all other thoughts
from my mind.

In the living quarters, the north hut, Matéo sat bolt
upright on a narrow folding chair. He looked miserable, frightened. I wanted to be alone and sent him
to his shelter in the hollow. He protested loudly and

sat down on the ground in the corridor outside, so I
shut the door and left him there. My headache had
returned, worse than before; my entire body seemed
one big ache.

Ten o'clock! Already the room looked like home.
Metal cases lined the walls; some of them were covered with bright blankets in red and cream and blue,
so they could be used as seats, others held books and
magazines. A mirror reflected the window and a

branch that swayed back and forth in the storm.
Wooden shelves, standing on glass bottles pounded
in the earthen floor as a protection against termites,
held bright pottery and glassware. Grandmother's
little clock—she started housekeeping with it, too—
ticked steadily away on a peg driven into the wattle-
and-daub wall; its weights ran up and down on
strings. There was the table with its white cloth, its
green orchids, and places laid for two. The pottery,
the linen, and the clock were the surprises for the
Duke from Captain Kidd's Treasure-Trove.

Eleven o'clock! A black and coral centipede
crawled lazily in and out of the thatch. Drip . . .
drip . . . went the rain on the roof. Tap . . . tap . . .
went the branch against the bamboo shutters. A red
wolf howled; another answered. The room which had
felt so cool, was stifling, but the rain blew in if I
opened the door.

Twelve o'clock! Tick . . . tock! Tick . . . tock!
said Grandmother's clock. Back and forth I paced,
from window to door, from door to window. Tick
. . . tock! jeered the clock. Tick . . . tock! Then it
changed its tune and I sang it over and over as I
walked. Hickory dickory dock . . . the Duke ran
up the clock . . . How silly of him! I laughed so
loudly that Matéo, frightened, peered in the door.

Then a girl came into the room. She annoyed me;
she did all the things I did. If I stopped, she stopped.
If I walked, she walked toward me, but we never

met. I scowled at her—tall, slim, so dark, with great
black hollows for eyes in a queer gaunt face; she
scowled back. I spoke to her, but the surf booming
on the shore made such a noise—or was the noise in
my ears—that I could not hear her answer.

One o'clock! Tick . . . tock! Tick . . . tock! The
Duke ran up the clock. What a silly thing to do.
So cold. Tick . . . tock! Something went around in
my head, around and around . . . Hickory dickory
. . . like a ball rolling . . . The Duke . . .

"Quick. Catch her!" said a voice a long way off.

". . . ran up the clock," I finished clearly, as the
ball exploded. Warm, thick blackness engulfed me.

I wakened from a deep sleep. With painful effort
I endeavored to look around, to find out where I
was. But my eyes, when I lifted the weary lids, were
unsteady and my vision dim. My limbs were heavy
with an infinite fatigue. Suddenly I caught sight of
someone's hand lying close beside me, a thin hand,
quite white, in which blue veins showed clearly. All
my perceptions were concentrated upon that strange
hand, so strange it might have been a foreign object
and so unlike my own—for mine was long and slim,
but brown and very strong. I decided to push the
hand away—I resented it, so near me, but with the
impulse the hand moved and I found it belonged
to me.

Matéo appeared within my range of vision. He stared at me, then called to someone whom I could not see, but before this other person arrived Matéo seemed to float away upon a great pink cloud. Once again I slept. And then I woke and slept again.

Just before dawn, one morning, I wakened with the feeling of new life flowing through me. I lay quietly, luxuriating in this sense of well-being, not thinking, content to be free of pain, of fatigue. My cot was in the corridor. A cool breeze swept through the rooms and, without moving my head, I could see a pale yellow film of light spread over the sky. On a sloping tree trunk two tiny green lizards met, bowed politely, made love, and vanished in the cashew thicket.

At my first move Matéo was beside me. I was pleased to see his real delight at my recognition of him. "The Duke?" I must have been very ill; my voice was only a whisper.

"He is here. Don't talk." Matéo's voice was kind. The Duke came quickly, but before I could ask him where he had been, Matéo held a glass to my parched lips and I drank thirstily of a strong, pungent herbal brew, then slept again, the question still unasked.

The next day I was better. The Duke cared for me as tenderly as a woman, but oddly enough, it was Matéo's great strength that gave me the most rest. He lifted me as easily and as carefully as he did the Duke's valuable transit.

Eventually I found out why the Duke was hours late. He wouldn't talk about it, because he thought he was responsible for my illness. Matéo was much annoyed. He said I had jungle fever from the bite of a tick; any unknown fever in the tropics is called jungle fever. "Nothing to fuss about," he barked at my husband. "What's one woman more or less, anyway." But he told me the story of that stormy night.

Mounted on Moro, his dappled gray, my husband started for home at sunup; the baggage cart, driven by Montiel, followed. The country was open, with only the deep valleys flooded, and, although there was no trail, they expected to make the fifteen-mile trip in about five hours. Occasionally the Duke took a bearing on his compass and they made good time for a few miles. Then one of the lead oxen slipped and broke his leg. Putting the animal out of misery, they fastened the other to the tail of the cart and went on. Two animals, instead of the customary four or six, made but little headway with the heavy wagon; even on level, firm ground they covered only two miles an hour. Late in the afternoon they bogged down in the shallows of a small, swift stream. By then it was raining heavily. Senhor and vaqueiro, as well as the beasts, were cold and exhausted. The Duke could not ride on to camp for help, as Montiel refused to stay alone, fearful of haunts and tigers. Eventually they pried the wheels out and, laboring through the dark, reached camp at length, almost at the moment that I slid over the edge into delirium.

Chocolate as it grows wild in the Brazilian jungle.

Upper Left: Type of machete used in cutting primeval jungle. *Upper Right:* Adobe house showing typical native thatch. *Lower:* Tapir at bay; these animals are prized as food in Matto Grosso and other parts of Brazil.

Dom Candido was very busy. He was building a
shower bath against the back of the south hut. Much
to his obvious disgust, I was overseeing the job. The
Duke was at work. He rode out with his crew each
morning and returned home each night. I felt guilty
at costing him so much in time and effort, but he
refused to leave me alone and I was not well enough
to go into temporary camp.

The shower bath was elegant—a real luxury. A
circular enclosure of split palm trunks was roofed
with leaves from the same kind of palm. A bamboo
door closed the entrance. Light entered between the
cracks in the palm-wood uprights. Ropes, a pulley,
and a five-gallon kerosene tin formed a crude but
effective shower. Months later I thought of it with
longing; my bath then was a quick rub with kerosene, to remove chigoes and other vermin acquired
during the day.

As soon as the shower was finished I decided to
build a chicken pen, something on the order of the
kitchen, only not so large, and enclosed on four sides.
The kitchen was made of split palm, roofed over,
with a four-inch space between roof and siding for
the smoke to escape. Ordinarily it would have been
an open shelter, with a fire built in the middle of
the floor, but I liked to try my hand at cooking,
occasionally, and objected to so much exposure. I got
over that habit, too. The cooking utensils, except the
iron Dutch oven, were of aluminum, for lightness.
Weight is so important that we carried only absolute

essentials, such as a coffee pot, three kettles, spoons and forks, a small meat grinder, a tiny coffee mill, and a half-dozen kitchen knives. My fripperies were taken along under protest. The Dutch oven was most important; in it we cooked the inevitable black beans which are a part of both meals—the eleven o'clock breakfast and dinner at seven. These beans, to be well-cooked, must be started in the evening over a slow fire, which is kept burning all night; they are thus warm enough for breakfast and the remainder is reheated for dinner.

Matéo was down at the lagoon, finishing a tiny raft on which I could sit, or stand and pole myself along the shores. The lagoon was increasing in size day by day, as more and more land became flooded; in the dry season it was only a small body of water. He looked up and I waved to him; we needed fresh meat badly. Furthermore I was bored just bossing Dom Candido. I left him busily at work on the chicken pen, had Julio saddle Tiger and started down the hill. Matéo's Onça was cropping grass near his master—a gaucho seldom walks.

Tiger hesitated a moment at the brink of the hill and I gave him a little kick with the stirrup to start him off. To my amazement he squatted on his haunches, forefeet braced, and slid down so swiftly I nearly fell backward, only saving myself by clutching him firmly around the neck. The wet grassy slope was slippery as glass.

Matéo was waiting at the bottom of the hill. His rifle, a Winchester 44, lay across his saddle.

Queer rumblings confirmed my suspicions and I scowled at him ferociously, whereupon the rumble burst into a laugh that shook him as malaria shakes its victims. After a moment I laughed, too, a trifle sheepishly, it may be. I remembered the Jesus Christ bird episode, about which he had never rebuked me, nor mentioned it to the Duke. Since then we had been better friends, although our relationship still left much to be desired. But danger shared always draws people closer together, even as the gift of laughter, which we both enjoyed, proved a common denominator.

Of late he had done many kind deeds. The gaucho boasted that he beat his three women every day so that they would sympathize with each other and live in harmony. Yet he rode often into camp with white, gold or crimson orchids twined around his hat, because the Senhora Boss liked them. And when I was so very ill, the Duke said that Matéo carried Mae West to me, thinking I might notice the hen of which I was so fond; Matéo hated the chickens. Because of things like this I did not begrudge him the fun of seeing me wrapped around my horse's neck.

Matéo finished his laugh and wiped the tears from his face with the red cotton scarf hung around his neck. It did duty also as a sweat cloth for his face. He gave a hitch to the fringed leather apron which protected his legs from thorns and rode off at a brisk canter along the edge of the lagoon, which was separated from the jungle by a narrow strip of land on which grew stunted, thorny plants; at evening all kinds of wild animals would cross it silently to drink. I followed slowly, trying to decipher the tracks that dappled the sand. They fascinated me.

The sound of a shot caused me to start guiltily. I had wasted time looking at the tracks and had quite lost sight of Matéo. The pulverins, tiny black flies the size of midges, began to attack in full force; they got into my eyes, my ears, and tried to crawl up my nostrils. I rode swiftly to the foot of the hill, where Matéo joined me, carrying the carcass of a veado which had thought itself well-concealed by the reeds.

It was nearly dark. As my horse scrambled over the brow of the hill, I glanced over my shoulder at the sunset. A glory of color swept the sky—from dull copper to orange and crimson, verdant green to Prussian blue—to merge at last into subtle tints of mauve and amethyst. I rode on home.

The house and the cooking fire, like all lonely dwellings and all lonely lights, looked self-reliant. "Like those on the plains back home," I thought, remembering how I always raised the shade in a Pullman berth so that I could watch the widely separated specks of light push back the darkness surrounding them. I shoved aside the mosquito cloth and entered the corridor. The Duke was not yet home.

The last light shone on our hammocks, hanging

limply on their hooks, packing cases upended near
the walls, and on all the odds and ends pertaining to
camp life in the jungle that were piled between them.
Gradually the noises of the day gave place to the more
mysterious sounds of the night. The nerve-shattering
howl of a maned red wolf came from the forest beside me.

From the shelters in the hollow, the smoke of many
fires drifted in thin gray columns; the vaqueiros,
waiting for their comrades, lay sprawled full-length
about the glowing embers of the palm boles, resting
from the heat of the day. After the evening meal
they would sleep, wrapped like cocoons in their saddle cloths, with their feet to the fire, in hollows dug
in the sand.

Matéo, busy around his fire, started toward the
house. His spurs clinking as he walked announced his
coming; in one hand he carried a flashlight and in
the other a kerosene tin filled with hot water. He
always sang as he worked and tonight was no exception, although the song—about the nun who fell in
love with a gaucho—was new to me:

> "For though the convent rule was strict and tight,
> She had her exits and her entrances by night."

he warbled lustily, as he dropped the flash and set
the tin of hot water on my dressing table. He began
to straighten the furnishings of the huts; this was
not his job, but he was very jealous of any one else
doing anything for the Duke.

I smiled at the song as I bent to unlace my boots. No insult was intended. "You'll find the boys a tough lot," the Duke told me in Bahia. "They're hard riding, hard shooting, and hard living. You'd better think it over well. It's safer all round in the cities." "Who said anything about safety?" I jeered. "Live dangerously! That's my motto. I won't bother you a bit, you'll see. You'll never have to worry about me." It hadn't worked out quite that way, but I was learning fast.

Matéo finished his work and went to order the evening meal. Busy with my thoughts, I changed automatically to a loose white robe, a favorite of the Duke's, and soft leather Russian boots. I was careful never to step on the ground with my bare feet. Already I had made the acquaintance of carrapatos do chão, ticks related to the spiders; they are found on bushes and sometimes in the soil. In areas where they are common, it is the height of folly for travelers to slacken their vigilance. These ticks sink their probocis in the flesh and suck blood until their bodies swell to the size of a small narrow bean. We always inspected our entire body after a day in the field. The natives also are troubled by these pests and animals are not immune.

I looked at the clock. Nearly eight. I wished the Duke would come home. The house seemed large and lonely without him. I slipped into my hammock and swayed slowly back and forth. The songs of the

vaqueiros, the twang of their guitars, was loud above
the hush of evening. In a moment I was asleep.

Bang! Crash! The hammock, with a virtuous air,
turned over, landing me in a heap on the floor. I
righted it and climbed in again.

I was wide-awake. Eight-ten. Where was the
Duke? I was starved. Matéo came in, his hands filled
with purple orchids—tiny deep purple blooms with
a glowing crimson spot like blood on their lips; every
day I fell more deeply in love with these flowers, the
most highly specialized of all plants. Cauto set up
the folding table in the corridor—we ate there on
clear nights—and covered it with the pale-green oilcloth Matéo handed him. I watched Matéo with
amusement and joy—his hands seemed so awkward,
but they were deft and swift; his color sense was
marvelous and the purple orchids in the low green
bowl were exquisitely arranged, better than I could
have done.

Cauto looks like a pirate, I thought idly. All the
vaqueiros did, in fact—unkempt black hair, huge felt
hats, usually pinned up in front with thorns, red or
blue ragged shirts, short pants, fringed leather aprons,
bare feet and legs, and long clanking spurs. Some of
the Portuguese Brazilians wore gold hoops swinging
from their ears. All had knives stuck in their wide
leather belts. Matto Grosso is still South America's
wild West.

Suddenly an agonized wail smote the darkness.

Deep-pitched, prolonged and horrible it reverberated through the house. Again it sounded . . .

"Yo-yo-ho-ho-ho-wah!"

Stunned, I held my breath in fright. Matéo and Cauto looked at each other; the vaqueiro crossed himself. "Haunts," he whispered to Matéo.

"Yo-yo-ho-ho-ho-wah!"

The place is haunted, I thought; the noise seemed to come from the bedroom. Matéo snatched his gun from its holster and, with me as a quaking rear guard, entered the room. All was serene, silent. There was no intruder. Again the queer cry. He stepped outside, pushed open the shower-room door and turned the light of the flash on the floor.

In the lighted circle squatted a frog of unbelievable size, form, and color. It was as large as a small plate. Its sides were so fat and round that it appeared circular in shape. Its enormous mouth sloped downward at the corners, like that of some grim, bad-tempered old man. Its skin was a dusky brown, covered with big rusty-looking greenish patches; horns decorated the top of its head. I gaped at it in astonishment.

Matéo prodded the creature gently with a stick. It swelled to twice its size, opened its mouth, and gave voice to a long wailing screech. We smiled at each other in relief. Once the light was removed from

it, the frog hopped for the security of the cashew
thicket.

A few minutes later there was the sound of men's
voices—shouts, laughter. "Company," said Matéo,
smiling broadly. I ran to the door. From the depth
of the forest appeared two horsemen carrying flaming torches. A hide-covered carreta followed, piled
high with tents, baggage, and supplies. The cart was
drawn by three pairs of snow-white oxen. A stranger,
my husband, and his crew rode behind it.

So that explained Matéo's attention to the dinner!

Excited, but a little annoyed, I rushed to the mirror
to see how I looked. Even in the jungle, I decided, a
wife has a right to know when guests are coming.
The Duke had known, of course, but he wanted to
surprise me. He had! The mirror showed sleek black
hair, a face still thin and pale from illness, a clinging
white gown—really a negligee—and scarlet leather
boots. "Not so bad," I thought complacently, although I really am not vain—not more than most
women, anyway.

Once upon a time I was very partial to blondes—
my roommate in school had long golden curls and
a real peaches-and-cream complexion. We both had
a crush on the same boy. I thought yellow hair and
a lovely skin gave her the edge on me, so I soaked
my black locks in peroxide and stole the cream from
the top of the milk bottles to use as a face wash. I
had heard that these ingredients were marvelous aids
to beauty. Sent home looking like a picked chicken,

my brittle, streaked locks cut close to my head, I skulked around until they grew out a bit. After that disastrous attempt, I left well enough alone. As I grew up, I found a lot of things could be done with black hair and a dark complexion!

Matéo raised the mosquito cloth with a flourish. He liked company—especially the company of an important man. And this stranger, Dom João Barros, my husband's employer, was important. Pride of race, pride of family, pride of power—all were evident in his careless stride, his quick flashing smile as he bent over my hand. "Estimo do conhecelo, Senhora." He was over seventy, but carried his years lightly. Born in the tropics, he looked more like a Minnesota farmer than the owner of immense cattle fazendas in Brazil and the Argentine; although a great-grandfather, he still wanted to increase his holdings.

"Camp life de luxe," the Duke mocked as we sat at dinner. But his eyes were proud as they roved over the green oilcloth, the silver, the pottery, and the deep purple of the orchids. It did make a difference. Dom João murmured polite nothings and stroked his full white mustache, but he took second helpings of all the well-cooked and well-served dishes.

Cauto and Julio, under Matéo's guidance, had outdone themselves. I felt slightly envious as one perfect dish after another was passed around. I could never do as well. Matéo, beaming with patriarchal pride, stood behind my chair; he refused to eat until we were through.

The soup tureen—a shining aluminum kettle from
the kitchen—was placed before me and I ladled out
generous bowls of canja, a sort of chicken soup made
with rice and spices—canja is derived from the word
kanji, meaning a thick rice soup enriched with
chicken and condiments. It was introduced into
Brazil from the Portuguese colony of Zoa in southern
India. Then came the pièce de résistance, an immense
platter of churrasco, broiled beef in other words,
served with black beans and rice; delicious buttered
noodles are usually served with churrasco, but we
had neither white flour nor rolling pins. The salad
was exotic—wild avocados, the pits removed, the
meat minced with bottled olives, red peppers and
olive oil, and replaced in the green shells; hearts of
palm—delicate and nutty in flavor—were sliced on
the side of the plates. Caxaca, the fiery native rum,
was served with the meal. It is almost as indispensable
as mandioca meal.

This in itself was a meal for a king, but Matéo
ushered in, with great pride, huge steaks of venison
and capybara, and a pot filled with a delicious stew,
which proved to be made of young monkey, cooked
whole, then disjointed; the tiny crumpled paws looked
so human that I lost my appetite for stew.

It was not until the dessert, sold in Brazilian shops
as egg threads or fios de ovas, was served that I
thought of the chickens. (The dessert is made of
shredded cocoanut—dried or fresh, sugar, and eggs.)
With horror I remembered the chicken soup I had

eaten with such relish. Where did Matéo get the chicken!

Rising hurriedly, I excused myself and, taking my flashlight, started for the new chicken pen Dom Candido had finished only that afternoon. Matéo slid unobtrusively into the night. Dom João and my husband, noticing my agitation, left their coffee and followed. Dom Candido was there, fussing around his architectural creation. I unfastened the door and peered within. My light shone on two sleepy hens. Of Brigham there was no sign.

I wept with rage, leaning against the side of the pen. The Duke said nothing, leaving me to solve the problem in my own way. Dom João stroked his mustache and murmured sweet nothings—at least, I hoped that's what they were—into my ear. I turned to him for sympathy and found him shaking with laughter, his flashlight casting weird shadows as it wavered in his trembling hand. I followed his glance and for the first time actually saw my chicken pen.

It looked like the leaning tower of Pisa!

Seeing our attention riveted on the pen, Dom Candido beamed with pride. I saw nothing to be proud of, or to laugh at, either, although Dom João and my husband bent double, snorting and choking with glee. When he could straighten up, the Duke held a tape on the pen. Not only was it out of alignment, but one side was three feet longer than the other.

"Why on earth," he asked Dom Candido, exasperation creeping into his voice, "did you make one side longer than the other?"

"Poco mas o menos," the great engineer answered, with a shrug. A little more or less—what matter?

From that day on everything he did was "poco mas o menos."

So we called him Dom Poco-mas, for short.

Chapter Eight

MY COUNTRY HOUSE

*January summer—A tropical garden—The raft—
Jungle journey—"Your country house awaits"*

JANUARY SUMMER, that year, came in February. Each
year in Matto Grosso, during the rains, there is a
break—an intermission of two weeks of bright, sunny
weather. Usually it comes in January, thus its name.

The Duke and his men pushed ahead with the near-
by surveys. Dom Poco-mas fished and enjoyed himself; every night he brought me an offering of a fish
or a flower, much to Matéo's disgust. After Dom
João left, Matéo and I patched up our feud, he because he had paid me out, and I because I couldn't
think of anything to do to him.

In the cool of the day I worked in my tropical
garden. I had no idea of what would grow and what
would not, but I planted and transplanted and had
a grand time experimenting. Ever since I was a child
I've liked gardening.

I inherited a natural liking for the land. Mother's

Dutch ancestors settled large sections of the country near my birthplace and although Dad had no deep roots in this soil, as his people are scattered over Europe, when he married Mother he settled down to raising crops, chickens, race horses, making horse-shoes, and other occupations.

My maternal grandmother was a handsome woman, with high, rosy color and masses of bright-brown hair; at her death, at sixty-eight, it was still brown and shining. She dressed in shades of gray, with a white fichu folded round her neck. Always the stem of some lovely blossom was drawn through the onyx brooch that held her scarf in place. She herself tended her fragrant garden, with its variety of blooms, from old-fashioned pinks and "pineys" to the newest hybrid rose.

I inherited from Grandmother her knack with flowers. One corner of our garden at home was so shaded by the branches of a huge greening apple tree that it was useless for growing anything except shade-tolerant plants. I was only a tiny person when she marked off this corner and turned it over to me for my individual use. I moved bloodroot, Dutchman's breeches, and wild orchids—even today considered hard to transplant—in full bloom; and so rich was the soil, so faithfully were they watered, with rain water swiped from Dad's rain barrel by the barn, that it was a most unusual thing to have one wilt.

Grandmother would have been wild with envy if she could have seen my tropical garden. At home I

coaxed and sprayed and watered to get the plants I
wanted; here I pruned and pruned and literally tore
up by the roots magnificent flowers, in order that
the few I must have could survive. No fertilizers
are needed. The jungle growth covers more in a night
than one can prune in a week.

Though I knew my home in Matto Grosso—the
home of an engineer's wife—was only a temporary
one, I spent two hours in the early morning of every
fair day grubbing out weeds around the wild pineapples and setting out hibiscus bushes I had bought
and carried from São Paulo. The pineapples throve
and bore fruits; the hibiscus blossomed prolifically,
great blooms of crimson, pink, and white. I had Easter
lilies, gladioli, agapantos—blue blossoms resembling
arum lilies—sunflowers, dahlias, violets, mignonette,
and cosmos that grew more than ten feet high.

But the wild plants of the jungle were even more
beautiful.

During my convalescence from jungle fever the
little raft Matéo had built for me became almost a
second home. At first, protected by headnet and
gloves, I used it as an escape—an escape from the
jungle that closed me in, that seemed like an enemy,
a beautiful, deadly, fascinating enemy from whom I
could not get away. The Duke was busy in the field
all day. The evenings, with him home, were perfect,
but the days—once the newness wore off—were too

long. I was not strong enough to ride or start a garden. We had no mail, no new books, no magazines, no papers. In the jungle, more alluring than any book, fever lay in wait for me.

After January summer the heavy rains began. Always there was a steady drip, drip from the leaves of the forest trees, dripping onto black leafmold rotten since the beginning of the world. Crimson, blue, and orange patches of mold covered the brown of the palm thatch. Armies of ants swarmed relentlessly up the walls of the huts, repelling with stinging bites all attempts to remove them. My clothes were damp, as was my linen; that is, what there was left of it after the vaqueiros washed it in the muddy lagoon and pounded out the dirt with sticks.

I didn't want the Duke to know how bored I was. I spent every sunny hour on the lagoon, poling from one bank to the other. On the water I did not feel so shut in. But, gradually, the eerie jungle cast its fascinating spell upon me; its poetic beauty, its wildness, its unknown possibilities took hold of my imagination. Under its lure my fears evaporated. I carried paints, pencils, and notebooks to the raft. I spent hours copying flowers, matching exactly, with infinite pains, their delicate shadings; I watched closely birds, beasts, and even snakes, drawing them and making copious notes on their habits. Later, I bought books to identify the species I did not know; not all my specimens are in them.

Thus I started what is now my profession. Always

I liked to write, to draw, to paint. But Grandmother
—shrewd, canny Dutch Grandmother—believed people should live before all else. So I never published
anything until I was thirty. For years I relied entirely
upon my sketches to recreate the color, the face of a
foreign land. But of late I have added a small camera,
with an excellent lens, to my field equipment and I
consider it invaluable. Without it I should have been
unable to furnish the illustrator of *Suwannee River*
with photographs from which to make his sketches;
the swamp folk are suspicious and will not pose for
their pictures. A small camera, quick in action, provides the answer to such problems.

Only one small section of land remained to be
surveyed. The Duke had left it to the last, because
it necessitated his being away from home for about
three weeks. At last, when he could put it off no
longer, he broached the subject one night at dinner.

The sky was clear, with stars beginning to twinkle
in its blueness. From a moon vine, cascading fifty feet
or more from the topmost branch of an unknown
jungle tree, was wafted a sweet, a cloying smell that
drugged the senses. I felt happy, at ease, content with
the world.

But I was not so contented that I was going to
stay home alone for three weeks, if I could possibly
go along. So I said, in a pleased voice, "Grand, I've

been wanting a trip into the wilds. Life in a city apartment is a little monotonous."

The Duke looked worried. "I don't see how I can take you," he said. "We have to pass through real jungle country; we won't use the cart. That means no tent, no comforts of any sort, and the food will be very poor."

But I was determined. I went.

I shall never forget that journey. I remember it with horror and loathing.

We left early the following morning, striking east by southeast toward the Rio Sepotuba. Matéo and four vaqueiros led the way, cutting and slashing at the matted jungle growth with their keen machetes. Dom Candido followed, leading a pack horse laden with instruments and our small supply of food; we practically would live off the country. The Duke and I rode last.

Some of the flooded land was uncomfortably swampy; Moro bogged down and his saddle had to be removed before he could be pried out. Tiger became frightened at a swimming water snake, and I had to dismount and lead him through the shallow pool. In marshy spots the plants, bamboos, scrub palms, and wild caete rushes, grew higher than our heads, even when we were on horseback. Hordes of fire ants swarmed on the bushes and, if brushed against, burned the skin like red-hot coals; tiny blisters and sores remained. Mosquitoes droned about us; their song was worse than their bite.

The day seemed endless.

No matter where we turned, we were confronted with an endless wall, an almost impenetrable wall of jungle. We proceeded slowly, carefully, for poisonous snakes crawled on the dark rotted leaves of the forest floor and lay coiled upon shrubs and branches; occasionally one, frightened by our nearness, would lose its hold and fall to the ground. At each step the horses sank ankle-deep in the soft, foul-smelling ooze. The air was thick with the odor of dead and decaying vegetation.

Every hour we stopped for leech inspection. These disgusting worms drop from the thickets and attach themselves to any exposed portion of the body. Their attack is usually unfelt, so that the clammy creatures suck blood until they become so bloated they can hold no more. Although leeches do no violent injury to the body, they weaken a person through loss of blood and thus make him less resistant to jungle fevers.

The weather, which had been threatening all day, finally made up its mind. The rain poured down in blinding sheets; we could see only a few feet ahead of us.

Suddenly we came into a narrow path, where wind-swept branches interlocked above to form a natural corridor. We pressed on, hurrying to find a clearing where we could make a leaf shelter for the night. Dark, fantastic trees, such as are found only in tropical jungles, lined the way. Tiny bats flitted in

and out between them. Matéo, leading, called sharply
to the Duke. We hurried up.

A solitary hut, primitive and wretched, was built
at the end of the natural path. The hut was dark
and deserted. Gray ashes from a long-dead fire lay

in a tiny heap in the center of the earthen floor; the
bones of some tiny jungle creature shone white and
glistening in a corner. Spiders, their loathsome bodies
curled into gray balls, hung quietly in fantastically
beautiful webs, waiting for unsuspecting prey.

I ducked in quickly, out of the storm. I ducked
right out again. The hut was *not* deserted.

The instant I stepped over the threshold a big

green lizard streaked between my boots; another fell with a plop to the floor. In the palm-thatched roof lived scorpions, three-inch cockroaches (I remembered the Duke's warning about the soup), toads, and even a brown and black snake. Matéo said the snake was harmless. Maybe so, but it put out its tongue and hissed, anyway.

I declared I wouldn't sleep in such a place. The Duke was in despair. He argued, he pleaded, finally he swore. I wept, but was firm. Matéo looked on in silence. Finally he could stand it no longer.

He killed the snake, stretched two saddle blankets under the ceiling so they would catch anything that fell, and made up my bed. I sat, sulky but righteous, out in the rain. If they wouldn't build a new shelter, all right, I'd get wet and die. Then they'd be sorry! But sleep in that hut I would not.

Matéo stalked out of the hut like an avenging angel. I had hurt his beloved Boss. "Madam," he sneered, "your country house awaits." Without waiting for an answer he grabbed me under his arm, stalked inside in the same dignified manner, and dumped me unceremoniously in a nest of blankets. Such a speech from Matéo! "Association with engineers has done you no good," I thought, but I said nothing aloud. After all, it *was* warm and dry inside.

I heard the Duke saying something quietly to Matéo and the gaucho's rumble in reply. Then, loudly—for my benefit, of course—"Treat 'em rough, Boss. They love it."

Below us roared the swollen stream, its clouded amber foaming into milky combers over every hidden jagged rock. We halted, dismayed, on the brink.

For days we had cut through thorn thickets and waded flooded marshes. Now, with our objective in sight—the last remaining plot to be surveyed—we could find no way across the river but a swinging monkey bridge of vines.

We had to cross. Without the angles and distances obtained from a survey of the small section across that river, the Duke could not close his traverse. His project would be a failure and we would lose all the money we had invested in it. We had received a retainer and a modest advance for expenses, but the final payment would not be made until the end of the job. No complete report, no money.

The sheer banks of red clay, saturate and slippery with the rains, dangerously eroded, were almost as difficult of passage as the river itself. The only solid objects anywhere were the two great fig trees, one on either side of the river and each some twenty feet back from the bank, around the roots of which the rotted lianas of the swinging bridge were tied. The terrestrial roots of the figs, as always, spread out near the surface. Uncovered by the rains, it seemed to me that even they held very fragile tenure upon the crumbling soil; only their tough aerial roots held them upright.

Hung in an arc between the two trees, the woven

bridge swayed slightly in the quivering air above the river.

Matéo slid down the bank until he could reach the lianas. He suspended his whole weight from the bridge, to test it. That was his job. "Snap, snap," over the roar of the river; "ping-ng-pin-ng," as the fibers parted and curled back like corkscrews. Not a vaqueiro would risk crossing after that.

I looked meaningly at Dom Poco-mas, the lightest man in the outfit. He could carry over a light rope, pull the heavy one after him, fasten it, and return— hand over hand—before he made camp to await our return. But *that* daring engineer turned his back on the bridge, spat around his one tooth, and sat down with finality.

The Duke was silent, as usual. He walked to the brink and looked down at the roaring current. "Well, we gambled and we lost," he said briefly; but I knew his heartsick despair. "We'll *have* to turn back."

Chapter Nine

THE MONKEY BRIDGE

*The lightest "man"—Bridge of vines—Breaking
lianas—"Just like a woman"—The fifty-foot snake
—The plateau—Home again—Dom Poco-mas'
women—Last day in my first home—The Missionary
—Until death*

THE REPORT OF the survey could not be finished.
Everything that we had staked on this reconnaissance
would be gone. Matéo was glowering; he idolized
the Boss.

"You don't weigh anything, Senhora Boss," he said,
"that bridge would hold two of you." He waited for
the suggestion to sink in and his sidewise glance was
eloquent. What kind of a wife was I, anyway, to
let my husband's whole project fail, almost at the
end, with close to $3,000 sunk in food, pay, equip-
ment, when I could cross, carrying the hand line
which would swing the men over in safety?

I had, as a matter of fact, already decided that I
would go. I have a good sense of balance. I am not

troubled by high places. I motioned to Matéo and quickly he tied the slim rope about my waist. I was already on the narrow swaying vine bridge, steadying myself by the rail lianas, before the Duke saw what I was doing. He made a gesture to draw me back, but he could not reach me. After all, if Matéo said the bridge would hold me . . . it would *hold* me. Matéo would take no chances with the Senhor Boss's woman, worthless though she be.

The bridge sank down beneath my weight, light as I was, but I stepped out over the water. It was scarcely five feet above the swollen river. Tussocks of grass, broken branches, a dead alligator, swept careening by below me. A third of the way over the hammocklike propensities of the swinging bridge nearly made me lose my balance. I tottered, almost pitched over the vine handguard. Recovering, I stood for a moment looking down. A small island of bunch grass and shrub came merrily along over the combers, as if riding a roller coaster. As it passed beneath the monkey bridge, I looked into the cold black eyes of a snake coiled snugly there in the center. Pieces of the bank were constantly breaking away and tumbling into the water, darkening its muddy amber.

Once more steady, I stepped quickly but cautiously forward. Midstream, twenty-five feet from either shore . . . suddenly, "Cree-eeck, crack . . ." the wet vines stretched to their utmost and began to part. "Ping-pi-i-i-ng-ng." The bridge beneath my feet sank to its lowest point. I was within a foot or two of the racing water. It was probably not more than five or six feet deep even at flood tide, but a man could not stand in a foot of that racing current and keep his balance. Paralyzed with fear, I stopped dead when I should have kept running forward. There I hung suspended over the roar; voices from the bank were lost in the voice of the river.

Then a curious thing happened. Through my mind there flashed a vivid recollection of myself as a child, hanging thus over a terrible void, scared, helpless. A great fright which I had had long ago was the thing that was paralyzing me now. I was about ten when my cousin persuaded me to hang onto the bell up in the church steeple, while he pulled the rope and swung me and the bell from below.

When the bell tolled suddenly, he became terrified lest the people should come hurrying to the church to find out what was the matter. He dropped the rope and ran, leaving me swinging in space atop the bell, some thirty-five feet above the vestibule flooring. Too far from the platform at the top of the steeple ladder to jump down to it, I clung frantically to the bell rope. As the clangor died away, the old rope, unequal to my added weight, began to part. I could hear the strands snapping, one by one. The horrible sensation of that moment of waiting was relieved now as I hung over the muddy Sepotuba, waiting for the last vine of the bridge to snap.

There was no bell rope here on which I could slide down to safety, as I had then, trembling, ill, the palms

of my hands rope-burned, otherwise unhurt—A
hoarse bellow from the bank brought me sharply
back to the present . . . profanity, violent, unin-
hibited. . . .

"Just like a woman," Matéo's shouts reached me,
"sticking there." Then something like "Never knew
one who could finish what she started!"

I was furious. On hands and knees I began to crawl
up the bridge towards the opposite bank. Foot by
foot I went forward. The bridge still held, shaking,
by one slim vine. Five feet . . . ten . . . fifteen . . .
twenty; just ahead was the mud of the far bank. I
was on firm soil. I stood up and reached out for the
anchoring aerial root of the great fig, the only tree
within hundreds of feet strong enough to support
bridge or guide rope. I must tie my rope securely
about that root.

Believe me or not, it does not change the fact, as
I reached out for that sturdy support I saw the only
great snake that I saw in all South America. It coiled
there, glistening, beautiful, a green-gold metallic
lusterlike lacquer over its lovely pattern of spots and
chains. Its subtle shades of reddish-brown had been
lost against the gray-brown fig root and the red-
brown clay of the bank; its glowing tail, almost a
blood red, had been concealed in the dark-green foliage of a twining passion vine; now it glowed in vivid,
wicked color above my head. It was a Brazilian
giboya, a land boa, that kills by squeezing its victim.

I ran back from the tree, stood perilously on the

brink of the crumbling bank, and, cupping my hands, screamed over the roar of the stream that I could not tie the rope because of the snake. How big was it?

"At least fifty feet long," I screeched, "almost two feet wide."

"Shoot it," the Duke shouted back. I had no gun on me, of course. The Duke knew that and intimated that he would send over to me on the guide rope his own pistol *in* the holster. I am a fairly good shot with my little 22 rifle. I can handle a shotgun, though the "kick" bruises my shoulder. But I am afraid of a revolver.

There was nothing else to do. I could not get back without anchoring the rope on this side of the bank. I pulled on the guide rope until the Duke's holster, with his Colt 38 inside, came into my hands.

"Point the *hole* at the snake!" Matéo's bellow came across the water. Flashes of rage at the implied insult came to my aid. There was nothing to do but cock it, hold the pistol in both hands and aim it at the beautiful deadly menace hanging there. I shut my eyes and pulled the trigger with both index fingers. As the shell exploded I promptly collapsed, sitting down incontinently in the mud.

The giboya fell in writhing coils to the ground. Aiming for the center of the mass, I accidentally shot it through the head. Its ruby tail flashed and curled and twisted; its colors faded, it lay still. Spurred on by the lusty cheers from the far bank, I pulled over the heavy rope and finally succeeded in tying it firmly

to the fig tree. Then I sat down to rest and watch the
men come over, pulling themselves hand over hand,
one foot set in a slipknot loop.

When they were all across the Duke measured the
snake. It was seventeen feet long. A scant six inches
in diameter, normally, this fellow, having just gorged,
really was nearly a foot across the middle. The
giboya does not attack man and this one would not
have bothered me, sleeping off his dinner as he was.
The Duke and Matéo roared with laughter. But I
refused to be ashamed. That snake certainly looked
fifty feet long to me. Anyway, I had gotten across
the bridge.

"Well, you surely made it, 'Tite," (which is the
Duke's nickname for me—short for Petite.) He pat-
ted me on the shoulder. "But Hell and Maria! You
had me fit to be tied for a minute."

Matéo growled something, I don't remember what;
yet somehow he gave me to understand, for the first
time, that there *might* be some use in a skinny
woman, after all.

Two days later we recrossed the Sepotuba. Rain
had fallen steadily and the river was higher than before. The men's feet dragged through the muddy
current as the foot sling swept down and along the
guide rope; each man hauled himself up hand over
hand to the far bank. I rode over on the Duke's
shoulders, my hand tangled in his thick hair; for the

first time I really became aware of the silver that
threaded its blackness. "Price of a wife," Matéo said
drily, when I remarked on it. He splashed across the
river like a porpoise holding tightly to the rope; the
last man over, it was his job to untie it. Rope is too
expensive to waste. Miles below this point horsemen
are sometimes ferried over or ride across on planks
placed on dugouts. There are few permanent bridges.

Dom Poco-mas had made a snug temporary camp.
We rested a day in the leaf shelters. The Duke and
Matéo spent the time consulting maps and records.
Matéo believed the high plateaus to be better cattle
country than this lower plain, even though there was
less water. Eventually the Duke decided to ride up
and look it over, and include his findings in the report, although it was not part of his assignment. Dom
João Barros was very wealthy and conceivably might
be interested in further details about this part of
Matto Grosso. Dom Poco-mas and three vaqueiros
went home. The fourth man stayed with us.

The following day at dawn, we started for the
Parecís Plateau. It was Matéo's idea to strike across
country and intercept the right-of-way cut through
by the Brazilian Telegraphic Commission. This would
mean easy traveling, but when we climbed up the last
steep pitch, the country before us was so open the
Duke decided against it. The telegraph line lay to the
east; to follow it would take us miles out of our way.

We had only such foods—coffee, sugar, a little
chocolate, maté, and a few pounds of rice and beans

—as we could carry in our saddlebags. At the last
stream Matéo filled two canvas water bags, holding
between four and five gallons apiece. Into each he
dropped a few chlorinated lime tablets. I drank only
boiled water and but little of that, having taken no
typhoid shots; in fact, I never took this precaution-
ary measure until I went to Mexico, when I was
inoculated against all such diseases. Typhoid and dysentery, two great scourges of the tropics, are controlled to a great extent by vaccines; yellow fever,
in most South American countries is practically
eliminated, although occasionally there is an outbreak
of a few cases. The mosquito which transmits this
disease often is carried to incredible distance by automobiles, trains and airplanes; experiments have shown
that they may even be brought by planes into the
United States.

On the plateau I realized for the first time how
people actually could starve to death in the tropics—
the tropics which my avid reading had led me to picture as teeming with wild life, fruits, and berries.
Certainly on the Paraguay and Sepotuba we had seen
and lived on game aplenty; on the highland plains,
I was appalled at its scarcity.

A few pampas deer, red or gray brockets, scurried
off before us; the red-coated ones were plainly visible
among the scattered, stunted trees of the chapadão,
a type of high, almost level plain typical of parts of
Matto Grosso. Matéo said these deer never travel in
herds, but always in pairs, the buck helping the doe

protect the young. I questioned him closely about this, as at home bucks leave the does immediately after the mating season. Here I saw my first ostrich, or rhea. These birds are protected by law. Pumas were common; we saw many tracks in the sand. At night, around the campfire, we heard the howling of wolves, but I never succeeded in catching a glimpse of these odd creatures, which are herbivorous as well as carnivorous.

We had expected to cross the divide between the basins of the Amazon and La Plata. Into this last river empty all the streams that flow south; those flowing north eventually reach the Amazon. This is due to the topography of Brazil, the interior being much higher than the coastal region. In the northeast the land slopes gently from sea level to approximately 3,000 feet on the plateaus, which are broken by ridges or serras, deserts and open plains. South of Espirito Santo State the rolling country extends to the coast; at Rio the jagged mountainous peaks rise steeply from the sea almost 3,500 feet. Southern Brazil is an ever-increasing stretch of level grassy land which merges eventually with the Argentine pampas. But the Brazilian highlands, even a few miles from the coast, slope to the west, so that all rivers having their origin in the Plan Alto must flow westward, until they unite with one or the other of the two principal streams.

We never reached the divide. Montiel, the vaqueiro, had for some days moved slowly and acted as if in pain, but denied it when questioned. Matéo, however, had finally insisted on knowing what was wrong. He came to the Duke late one evening and asked for the emergency kit. The vaqueiro's legs were raw and bleeding from the ankles nearly to his knees; he was wearing an old pair of the Duke's riding breeches, of which he was very proud, otherwise we would have discovered his condition before. Carrapatos do chão, the grayish ticks that live in the dust, had caused such an irritation by sucking his blood that a serious infection had set in. The Duke was worried. We left for home the next morning, having bandaged Montiel's legs as well as we could with strips torn from my old linen combination. We boiled the linen, let it cool, and dipped the strips in permanganate solution. We stopped every hour or so on the way to wet the bandages.

By the time we reached home the wounds were better, although in spots the flesh, a peculiar reddish-violet in color, had decayed almost to the bone. Montiel recovered, but for weeks could scarcely put his feet to the ground.

Home again! I felt as though I had been abroad on my honeymoon and was just returning. I was elated, so pleased to be with my silver, my dishes, and my paints and notebooks. I could hardly wait to inspect our home and make certain the ants hadn't eaten away the table legs, or the vines hadn't enclosed the

doors and windows. For all I knew the creepers might
have completely obliterated the entire house from
view.

Everything was perfect—as perfect as it could be
in the rainy season—flowers trimmed, windows free
of vines, roof patched, the hens clucking busily about
their business in the chicken pen.

Stepping out to watch the sunset, I looked down
the hill straight into Dom Poco-mas' hut. To my
amazement, I saw a woman sitting there before his
cooking fire, busily stirring a pot from which a wisp
of steam arose.

The strictest rule in camp was *no women*. The
Duke aided this by weekly doses of saltpeter, which
he himself secretly put into their food. Knowing the
rule, I turned to call the Duke's attention to the increase in Dom Poco-mas' ménage. Certainly he had
no wife, no woman, when we left. This one was very
much at home. While I hesitated, I saw another
female walk up the path from the lagoon, push back
one of the cowhides hung from the thatch as a windbreak, and step inside. From her dress, her indepen-
dent carriage, I surmised she was an Indian.

"For a snaggle-toothed, lean old reprobate he does
himself very well," I muttered aloud.

"Who does?" queried the Duke in amusement.

"Poco-mas," said I angrily. "He's got two Indian
women down there!" I looked at the Duke expect-
antly, thinking, of course, he'd do something. But,

no. He sat down and began to work on his report. It was Matéo's duty to carry out orders.

One woman was enough for any man, I thought. However, it seemed best to mind my own business, so I turned back into the corridor where Matéo had just finished laying the supper table. I said nothing to him; he had three at home.

The next day was beautiful, more like an Indian summer day in the States than a day in the tropics. I worked hard, trying to paint, sketch, and write descriptions of as many odd or beautiful things as I could. We would soon be leaving. The work was practically finished. I would never see my first jungle home again. There would be other homes, apartments in New York and in other cities, but never again one like this. And my chickens . . . they'd go native!

Feeling pretty low, I washed the paint from my brushes and stretched out in the hammock. Swinging idly back and forth, I glanced down the hill to Dom Poco-mas' house. Yes, there were the two women still, working at a little stone hearth. As I watched I caught the flutter of a red and white skirt behind a cowhide at the far side of the shelter.

This was too much for Dutch economy. How could we ever feed three extra mouths? I knew I was not minding my own business and I learned later that Matéo was wise enough to close his eyes to what he felt, under the circumstances, was a minor infraction. Swinging down the path, presently I stood before Dom Poco-mas' castle. I could see inside clearly, the shelter had no side walls other than an occasional hide windbreak, but etiquette forbade my noticing this, or entering without an invitation. I gave the customary greeting:

"O de casa!" Hello the house, in other words.

Dom Poco-mas' snaggle-toothed grin appeared cheshirelike at the place where the door should have been.

"It is rumored," I began severely, "that women have been seen around. One woman is enough for any man. *Two* is disgraceful. But three! I wouldn't have believed it of you."

He spread his hands wide. "Como no?" Why not?

Defeated, I turned back up the hill, but he called to me placatingly, in his soft-voiced Spanish. (He never spoke Portuguese except for names.)

"Senhora Boss! What is one or two women, poco

mas o menos—a little more or less? They mean nothing to me." He waved his hand airily. *"Fishing* is *my* passion!"*

Tomorrow was to be our last day in the grass house. I thought I couldn't bear it. I begged the Duke not to pack anything until the very last minute; I wanted to enjoy it as long as I could, to remember it in all its beauty. I knew the Duke hated to leave, too.

The Missionary rode into camp in time for eleven o'clock breakfast. The Duke and I had been making polite conversation, and we welcomed his appearance—at least, I did. The Missionary was a German, traveling from one small settlement or ranch house to another, doing whatever he could for the people, regardless of race or of creed.

We sat for a long time over our beans, our fowl, our coffee, talking about the country, its beauties and its possibilities. This last was my husband's chief interest in engineering, the opening up and subsequent development of new lands. "The stuff of which pioneers are made," I thought, as I watched his firm brown hands—small for a man, but so competent, so expressive. He was drawing a rough map on the oilcloth cover and I didn't stop him. What did it matter now? The Missionary, absorbed, leaned across the table to see more easily.

"Look!" the Duke said. "Here, and here, and here." He pointed to huge unsettled areas in Matto

Grosso and other Brazilian states. "This is the land of the future, the land of tomorrow. With the world so unsettled, the people so discontented since the war, with poverty and misery wherever one turns, colonization of fertile lands such as these must be the answer."

Matéo leaned against the wall, listening intently.

"This is excellent cattle country," the Duke continued. "The zebus, the red humped cattle, do well here; pasture is plentiful. They are not so subject to disease as other cattle and worming them once a month will keep them in fair condition." Matéo nodded agreement.

"How about human disease, typhoid, dysentery, malaria?" asked the Missionary. "Isn't that really what makes colonization so slow?"

"No. Lack of transportation," my husband answered promptly. "Once good roads are built, the country opened up, settlers will swarm in. It's just like the settling of the West in the United States, the firstcomers, the pioneers, won't have such an easy time. But the climate is good, especially on the plateau, the valleys are suitable for modern agricultural methods and, even in the rainy season, the land is more than livable. And science is finding ways to care for tropical disease, just as Butantan is breeding and distributing harmless snakes that kill poisonous ones. It's a magnificent country."

I left them still talking and went to take a last look at the lagoon. A tapir feeding among the rushes slid silently into the water and swam away, leaving a silvery trail behind it; in regions where they are seldom molested they feed either night or day.

As I was about to return I met the Missionary at the vaqueiros' camp; we walked up the hill together. "Pardon, madam," he said apologetically, in his stilted English, "I was very much interested in what your good husband said about colonization and in his constructive ideas. I take it that he is of a titled family himself?"

"The Duke?" For a moment I was bewildered. "Oh! That's just a nickname. But yes, his ancestors were of an old titled family; they were exiled long ago for religious differences. He knew so much of the family history, which had been handed down from father to son, and, when I first knew him, told me so many interesting stories about their old home, where the city of Buda-Pesth now stands—and then, too, he always had a certain way about him, it was in the blood, I presume—that to tease him I called him 'The Duke'. It seemed to fit somehow—his dignity, his air of authority, his ease in handling his men—and we've called him by it ever since."

Just then we heard Matéo's whistle and quickened our steps. More company.

A girl, a man, and a horse—all three so thin, so worn.

"Boas tardes, amigos, se Deus quizer." The boy greeted us with the customary salutation of the Matto Grossonee.

"Good afternoon, friends," we replied in kind. "Se Deus quizer—God protect you."

They had followed the Missionary so far, the boy explained. They wanted to get married, not just do as many settlers must; they had a little ranch arranged for, but they were Lutherans—no other Missionary would do. His thin face flushed hotly as he put his arm around the slight figure by his side. She looked like a child, exquisite blond head down-bent, face piteous with the tension of controlling trembling lips; lips that tried hard to be brave.

I knew what he meant. Many settlers in isolated regions see a Missionary or a priest but seldom. Sometimes years pass before a couple have a chance to marry; often the children of such unions are baptized at the time the marriage ceremony is performed.

The Duke's eyes met mine, but he said nothing; I swallowed hard. It was my last night in our first home, but . . . How could I be so selfish. Of course the Missionary would marry them. They'd have the best wedding we could arrange and the pack horse, too. Both of them on one horse—I couldn't let them go like that. The chickens . . . there were lots of things they could have. The Duke was generous. He'd arrange it.

"Dearly beloved . . ." How sweet, how young she looks, I thought. My pleated white chiffon night-dress, draped over a satin slip, looked like a bridal gown from Paris. How lucky I'd had a friend's wedding present in my trunk. One small hand even now caressed its clinging folds, the other held tenderly a cluster of purple and gold orchids that many a bride would have envied. Around the door of the living room the vaqueiros clustered, silent, intent. The room was very still. "If any man can show just cause . . . let him now speak . . ." Dom Poco-mas' face was puckered like a child about to shed unwilling tears.

"Wilt thou have this woman . . ." Behind the bride's head was a bower of snow, a flowering cloud of moon blossoms from a jungle vine. Matéo's work. For hours he had toiled, twined and twisted the fragrant creepers until the wall of the hut vanished beneath a glory of pure white stars. "Tick . . . tock! Tick . . . tock!" sang Grandmother's little clock. "Another bride. . . . Tick . . . tock! Tick . . . tock!"

I could just see the Duke, standing erect beside the bridegroom. The girl beside me looked as though some fairy wand had touched her face, taking away the lines of care and fear.

". . . for better, for worse," the Missionary's gentle voice spoke the familiar words as though he were recounting a miracle. ". . . in sickness and in health . . ." The bridegroom's dark head bent protectingly over the small fair one—

"Until death us do part . . ."

Chapter Ten

VOODOO FIRES IN RIO

*River of January—Rio—We lose the Patagonian job
—Diamond Jack, tropical tramp—Macumba—Drive
to Petropolis—Voodoo fire—Priest of the flame—
The white cock—The sacrifice*

SUCH A SCANDAL was caused by the Tordesillas
Treaty of 1494 that Francis I, King of France, asked
the Pope where he had found Adam's will. It was by
this same famous treaty that Spain and Portugal
calmly divided between them all lands to be discovered in the New World. The agreement, it might be
added, was entered into under a Spanish Pope.

Ten years after Columbus landed, a Portuguese,
Gonçalo Coelho, sailed into what he thought was the
mouth of a great river. He named the place River of
January (some historians believe that de Solis gave
the river this name, although the Brazilians favor
Coelho) and started a settlement at this spot. The
village was called Carioca—White Man's House, by
the Indians—and a resident of Rio today is still called
a Cariocan.

We think the present is all that matters; we are a
tremendously "contemporary" generation. But the
reason for the hatred between the Spanish and the
Portuguese—who are alike in customs, food, manners;
whose speech and blood spring from the same roots;
who for centuries have stood literally face to face—
goes back to that same Tordesillas Treaty. Although
Portugal received the right to all the territory east of
a delimited line, running due north and south one
hundred leagues west of the Azores, she thus won
nothing but Brazil; Portuguese, therefore, is spoken
only in that last country. The inhabitants of all other
mainland Latin-American countries speak Spanish—
with the exception, of course, of the native Indian
tribes.

We first saw Rio from an Ita boat, a steamer which
plies up and down the coast. It was summer in the
States, winter in Rio—glamorous, bewitching Rio!
Guanabara Bay, so startlingly beautiful that it is like
nothing else in the world, glowed with living, pulsing
color beneath the orange rays of the slowly rising
sun. The mists of night still cast their mantle round
the sleeping city.

Guided by red and blue signal lights, the boat
moved slowly into the ever-widening harbor. To the
left reared the magnificent cone of the Sugar Loaf,
the Pão de Azucar, apparently lashed to the earth by
cables. Tiny aerial cars, carrying passengers back and
forth to the summit, were already creeping up the
incline like fireflies.

The sun rose over the eastern hills. At their feet, facing Rio across three miles of blue water, lay the city of Nictheroy. The mount of Corcovado, the Hunchback, surmounted by a colossal figure of Christ—face to the east, arms outstretched to form a cross—loomed hugely into the heavens. Frigate birds wheeled overhead. To the right the spurs of Tijuca emerged from wisps of clouds, faintly pink; Tijuca, highest peak of the blue-green mountain range which follows the coast to Rio Grande do Sul.

We walked down the gangplank, through a pavilion, and into the Avenida Rio Branco, the Rue de la Paix of Rio. I was confused, amazed at the sights and sounds. The city seemed to me more Parisian than Paris itself; styles, laughter, sidewalk cafés, even language, for most Brazilians speak French as easily as their Portuguese. Yet Rio is distinctly herself and has made her own the best of European and North American customs.

I could scarcely believe that this was an old, long-settled place, or that Brazilian history antedates our own, even after we were established at a quiet, delightful little hotel in Copacabana, everything was so modern.

The Duke was expecting confirmation of his next job, a reconnaissance for a railway in Patagonia. But in the package of mail awaiting us came the information that the Patagonian job was off; at least for the present. He was put out. He had sent a message to Matéo to meet us in Patagonia. Matéo had a job help-

ing a trader cross the divide with a load of trade
goods. They were making for the nearest small river
leading to the Amazon and would embark on it in a
rubberman's boat for Manaos. From there he would
work his way to Comodoro Rivadavia and wait, if
we had not arrived as yet. Matéo would not allow the
Duke to pay his fare; certainly not as long as there
were rivers to carry him and boats to ride in. There
was no way we could reach him now.

We had hardly digested this news when Diamond
Jack showed up. Diamond Jack was an individual
who was, in the last analysis, a magnificent friend to
everyone but himself; a great splendid-looking blond
man, his high color caused by a network of broken
veins in his cheeks. He drank and caroused, his home
was wherever he lay his head at night; a typical "tropical tramp." Jack's favorite work—if he could be said
to favor work at all—was in the diamond fields.
Brazil has enough mines, almost untouched, to supply the world demand for these precious stones. Jack
was fond of my husband, with whom he had worked
at various times and, when he heard that the Patagonian trip was off, he hooked his arm through the
Duke's and they went away together, leaving me to
rest up, read, and see the city. There was a letter from
the Professor in my mail. I was delighted to hear from
him again. They would be in Honduras in the fall, he
wrote. Would we, by any chance, be in the vicinity
during that time? He would show me some beautiful
butterflies if we met in Honduras.

I went down to Copacabana Beach as soon as I had changed my clothes. Gay with suburban houses, awnings, parasols, and bathing tents, it was like a bit of Basque France. Rio proper is only a few minutes away through the vehicular tunnel beneath the butte back of the beach; shortly I was wandering over its extravagant mosaic pavements, in patterns varying from the ultramodern to an Arabian Night's dream, past palaces and palms, and gardens with fretted fountains. The jagged peaks and turrets of the Organ Mountains loomed fantastically above the city, casting irregular shadows like a scalloped purple awning over plaza and boulevard.

All this beauty was distracting for a little while, but I was thinking of the Duke, sensing the disturbance beneath his silence. I returned to the beach while the sun still rode high above the peaks. The walls of the old fortress, Santa Cruz, stood firm and majestic upon the narrow ridge of sloping rock. Less than a mile away was Fort São João, guarding the other side of the entrance to the bay. There lay the isle of Villegaignon where in 1555 Nicolas Durand de Villegaignon, vice-admiral of Brittany, landed six hundred Protestants and Catholics. He took possession of the island in the name of Henry II of France. The gray walls of the Naval Academy now rest upon this spot.

Arriving at the hotel, I found the Duke already there, talking with Jack, whose florid color was mounting over the long, cool drinks set before them.

"Well, 'Tite," the Duke came straight to the point.

"Jack has put me in touch with a good proposition—
short, but important. But it's back in the jungles—
Amazon—this time. Senhor Floresta da Silva, his old
boss, wants a man to look over and estimate the cost
of establishing a rubber camp—a good one, with
places fit for the men to live in, not just hovels stuck
up any which way. It's a bit out of my line, but it
would give a lot of men work." He looked keenly at
me. "I told him no; you've never really recovered
from that bout with the jungle fever and malaria's
bad up there. Unless . . ." he hesitated, "unless you'd
consider staying here until I finish. Or maybe you had
better go back home."

This was a long speech for the Duke. Before he
finished I had time to boil right up to the explosion
point.

"You just try leaving me here, Mr. Marmaduke,"
I raged at him. "If you think I'm going back home on
some little lousy steamer while you play tiddlywinks
up the Amazon, you're mistaken. You know I'm just
crazy to see all those orchids you talk about—and
don't know the names of," I added meanly.

"Disposition—terrible!" murmured Jack.

I took a long breath. "Besides, I can take just as
much quinine for malaria as you can. So there!" said
I triumphantly.

"When," said I to the Duke impatiently, "are we
going to see a macumba ceremony? We'll be up the
Amazon before you know it."

Upper: Many native huts are constructed of reed and daub, with thatch of straw; the gardens are walled to protect them from pigs and other animals. *Lower:* Jungle lizard sunning on a log.

Upper: Telegraph lines such as this connect hundreds of miles of jungle country with civilization. *Lower:* Fight between anaconda and crocodile. The crocodile lost.

He looked at me suspiciously. "Who told you about macumba?"

"Diamond Jack. Don't you remember? He offered to drive us to Petropolis any night."

"We are not going to drive forty miles to see some silly voodoo ceremony," said the Duke firmly. "Besides it's against the law."

"You needn't be so virtuous about it," I retorted. "You were anxious enough to see the Penetentes in New Mexico."

"That's different," remarked the master of the house, loftily.

It was nearly sundown when we reached Petropolis. The town, the summer capital, is locally called "City of Hydrangeas"; these shrubs cover parks, gardens, and hillsides with masses of heavy-headed blooms. There were thousands of other flowers—frangipani, azaleas, camellias, orchids—and hundreds of deep-green tree ferns.

Jack knew a witch doctor, a Negro, who held an important position in the terreiro, the macumba church. He had employed the man as helper on a number of jobs and was certain that for a small fee he could persuade the Negro to let us witness whatever ceremony might be performed that night. What it would be he did not know—it might be the "rites for the dead", when spirits are called back to give advice to the living or to torment some enemy; sometimes these spirits are asked to prescribe for ill children, or to give other beneficial aid.

"Is macumba the same type of voodoo practiced in Haiti?" I asked Jack. I had never been to Haiti.

"Much the same," he replied, "except that Brazilian Negroes do not worship the snake. African fetishism and superstitions, imported into the country with slaves from the Sudan and Bantu tribes, and perhaps from other tribes as well, have been combined with the crude spiritualism of the Indian. They practiced spiritualism as a form of religious worship long before white men discovered the country."

The Negro lived in the mountains toward Therezopolis. We drove for a while in silence. Great purple shadows, the color of quaresma blossoms, spread over the hills and covered the valleys.

I thought about what I'd heard—that most of their rites were termed despacho; witchcraft that supposedly induces death in the person upon whom the spell is laid. The Negroes, particularly the lower classes, believe in it implicitly. (Hugh Gibson, former Ambassador to Brazil, writes in his book *Rio,* that Haitian voodoo and macumba are similar, although the ritual is not the same. He says that macumba worshipers are addicted to sacrifices of animals, with music, drums, and so on. Further, Mr. Gibson states that macumba churches operate "more or less clandestinely in the suburbs of the federal district and the state of Rio de Janeiro.")

"Sambo," Jack said in his pleasant voice, "is quite a

character. He received his 'powers' in Bahia. That's
where the cult really originated; but it has spread
quite a bit now. Although the practice of it is illegal,
the police handle it carefully and wisely; too much
pressure and it could easily become a menace."

"Do you really believe in it?" asked the Duke,
curiously.

"Well," he laughed, sheepishly. "Yes and no. I've
seen some queer things. Maybe you will, too, before
the night is over."

We turned into a narrow lane; jungle walls pressed
in upon us. Strange shadows, blacker than the night,
stalked across the road.

"How do you know there'll be any ceremony tonight?" I asked.

"First night of the new moon," he replied briefly.
"Hear the drums!"

I did not hear anything but a lone bird, wailing. I
glanced at the Duke, who shook his head. But Jack
seemed so confident I believed in spite of myself. For
another ten minutes we drove slowly along the winding way. Creepers brushed our faces—the perfume of
their creamy panicles hung heavy on the night air.

Without realizing quite when it began, I became
conscious of sound—sound that seemed to come from
above me, from behind me, from just around the
bend. I touched the Duke. He heard it, too. We left
the car at the end of the lane; the beat of the drums
now was clearly audible. They did something odd to
my blood; they woke a rhythm in my pulse, quick-

ened my heartbeat, so that I kept opening my mouth and swallowing air to equalize the pressure against my eardrums, as one does in a tunnel or subway train.

Jack parted the creepers and led us along a tiny path that went down, down, always down. He walked as confidently as though he were on a highway. I stumbled along behind, often only the Duke's tight grasp on my arm held me upright. My black dress was soaked with perspiration. An unseen, ruthless shrub clawed off my hat and left a long scratch as a souvenir across one cheek. Something stung the Duke; he swore under his breath. After hours of torture—or so it seemed—we came to a tiny clearing; two palm fronds hung across the trail. "Wait," Jack said in a voice I scarcely recognized. He parted the leaves, walked across the glade and disappeared into the jungle on the other side. Above the hollow boom of the drums, louder now, close at hand, I heard the sound of falling water.

I was horribly afraid—afraid of the drums, afraid of the hot, almost fetid air, afraid of what I would see; even a bit afraid of Jack. "Let's go back," I chattered; my teeth clicked together as loudly as castanets.

Too late. Silent as a shadow, the big man glided across the glade, motioning us to follow. The path dipped steadily downward. We passed a cluster of mud huts, dark, deserted. Little owls sobbed out their weird calls; hoarse yells of monkeys competed with the drums and the piercing din of nocturnal insects.

A bat became entangled in my hair. I felt desperately ill at my contact with the loathsome flying mammal.

A small nude figure stepped into the path, now a mere tunnel, whose interlocking leafy branches overhead shut out the moon crescent. The figure spoke no word. Monotonous, powerful, the drums sang on: tom-tee-tom-tom, tom-tee-tom-tom called the little drums enticingly; boom-da-da, boom-da-da commanded the big bass drum.

I shivered in the warm air. Icy fingers chased each other up and down my back. "You asked for it," the Duke's silence seemed to say. I gritted my teeth and went on.

Light ahead. High, leaping flames that lighted a clearing ringed by jungle, flames whose eerie brightness obliterated the pale moonlight. I could see the mask of white paint covering the figure's face; grotesque bars of white decorated trunk and legs. I stifled a gasp as it held up a hand, palm outward, and the drums quickened their beat.

On and on flowed the pounding rhythm; the jungle vibrated to the thudding sound. It rose and fell and rose again—monotonous, exciting, always the same pitch, never higher, never lower. Under its mesmeric vibration we moved stiffly to places indicated by the painted figure—Jack's acquaintance.

A huge naked Negro crouched above a hollow log over which a hide of cow or pigskin was stretched tightly; he used a short wooden stick and the heel of his right hand to strike the deep booming notes.

Two young boys—also nude—forced weird peculiar
rhythm from the small drums by stroking them with
their fingers, their palms, or by tapping the hide
sharply with their fingertips.

Water poured steadily over a low rock on the far
side of the clearing. There a couple of dozen Negroes
and Negresses squatted to watch a supper laid out on

a white cloth on the ground; the food looked delicious. A cock's tail in the center seemed out of place.
I couldn't understand why the crowd seemed so
tense, so filled with emotion. They paid no attention
to the Duke and me; Jack apparently knew everyone and the witch doctor vouched for our presence.

Three girls, thin, angular, stark-naked except for
white cloth girdles and strings of dried seeds around
their ankles, moved with stiff jerky steps toward the
roaring fire. The witch doctor, a garland of vines so

twined they looked like horns upon his head, handed
to each girl two candles in wooden holders. Their
faces were blank, wooden, expressionless. A low
monotonous chanting came from their scarcely moving lips. As one being they bent to the fire, lighted
the candles; as one being they moved to the spread
cloth and placed the wax candles upon it. The drums
beat a furious rolling crescendo of sound; the girls
straightened as one being and moved their feet backward in a slow, careful pattern. The Negro doctor,
white paint glistening, moved nearer to the fire to
await their coming.

The crescent climbed over the strangler fig. As at a
signal, the drums ceased at once.

I was almost ill with excitement. The sensuous odor
of black, naked bodies, glistening with palm oil and
sweat, nauseated me. The worshipers swayed back
and forth, never moving their feet—keeping time to
a queer barbaric chant doubtless sung beside African
voodoo fires centuries ago. The big drum picked up
the rhythm. Boom . . . boom . . . boom . . .

A young boy glided to the fire. He threw a fine
powder on the blaze, which flamed higher and higher.
Strange lights of blue and green flickered over the
swaying forms of the girls, the grotesque figure of
the witch doctor, now holding a gleaming, wicked-
looking knife in his hand. Wild, savage, barbaric cries
broke from the watching crowd. Casually, as though
it were part of his ordinary life, Sambo walked
through the flames, reappeared, returned to his own

side of the fire. There was no odor of singeing hair, of scorching flesh, but from the fresh green vines twined round his head floated black wisps of smoke.

The boy stole silently from the shadows. A white cock was in his hands. The bird's head swayed from side to side, as though it, too, were hypnotized by the sound of the drum. The girls screamed, howled, tore off their girdles, bounded high in the air. Flames glinted on bloodshot eyes. Young bucks sprang into the lighted circle and danced with the young women; first one couple, then another, another, fled into the jungle.

Still the drum beat on . . . faster . . . faster. . . .

The knife swished through the air. The cock, headless, dropped to the ground. The head rolled into the fire. The drum was still. Prostrate on the earth, the crowd was silent, too. All lay motionless but the white bird. Sedately, with measured tread, it walked about the fire-lit circle. The smell of singed feathers from the burning head provided the last touch of horror, the last bit of unreality.

The Duke pulled me away. Half carrying, half leading, he helped me to the car.

All night the drumbeat pulsed in my ears as the dance of love and sacrifice continued. We were still waiting for Jack when dawn came over the mountain.

Chapter Eleven

LOVE LIFE OF AN ORCHID

The Amazon—Belém—The market—The Tapajoz—
Red-headed giant—"I'll show you orchids"—Bagpipes
in the jungle—Hymns for a madman—Thousands of
orchids—Love life of an orchid—Superstition—
Second grass hut—I acquire unwelcome guests—
Mandurucu village—Native esperanto—Couvade—
Santarem—Poor fish

FROM MY HAMMOCK, slung forward beneath the canvas awning, I could see far up the Amazon. Only a faint haze marked the horizon, where sky and water met. Behind me, shut from sight by the *Itaúba's* cabin and tiny wheelhouse—where the pilot and the Duke pored over maps and charts—lay the same misty line of demarcation between heaven and river. To the right and left, an incredible distance away, I knew were solid walls of jungle, where tall trees thrust their heads above a body of impenetrable creepers, hardwoods, and palms.

Five days out from Belém; two more days to San-

tarem and the Rio Tapajoz, where the Duke was to
begin his work—the work of estimating the cost of
locating and constructing an up-to-date rubber
camp. Engineering in the tropics is more diversified
in scope than in the States. Although it means added
dangers and hardships, it recompenses by an infinite
variety of experiences. In addition to usual engineering assignments, such as bridges, railroads, drainage
and irrigation, the tropical engineer may scout for
hardwoods, rubber, oil, or minerals; lay out plantations for bananas, pineapples, or citrus fruits; and
devise methods of transportation through jungles and
other terrain not encountered by engineers in the
States.

Long before we reached Santarem, I had made
friends with Ramondo, who wore with pride both a
black goatee and a long drooping mustache. The
caboclo was a first-class riverman, recommended by
Senhor da Silva. Blue cotton trousers and gray under-
shirt, open to show his hairy chest, comprised his
clothing; rain or shine, he never wore a hat. He
spoke both Portuguese and Lingoa geral, a language
adapted by the Jesuit missionaries; this last was most
important, as nearly all native tribes are familiar with
it. Lingoa geral is a combination of Portuguese, with
a base of Guaraní and various Indian dialects. But
Ramondo spoke no English, so we swapped. I'd touch
or point at something and name it; he would repeat
it in Portuguese. Gradually with the pick and choose
system, we arrived at a workable plan, so that with-

out too much wigwagging we could carry on a conversation of sorts.

It was July, the beginning of the dry season, which
on the lower Amazon usually lasts until January,
with a few rainy squalls in November. Many trees
flower in the dry spell. June and July are months of
great activity; the birds have finished molting, shrubs
are in bloom, and all the insects necessary for pollina-
tion appear simultaneously with the flowers.

We were practically on the equator but the nights
were cool and pleasant, the mornings almost cold.
The Amazon trade winds blew steadily upstream and
there was also a great amount of evaporation. But
when the sun stood overhead it was scorching. Yet
the Duke and I slept rolled in blankets.

Ramondo pointed out to me, whenever we were
close enough to see a shore, the low ridges where castanhas grow; the nuts, from trees more than a hundred feet high, ripen from March to April. Although
it was past the season, he brought a nut back from a
wood station; it resembled a husked coconut and the
hard shell—so hard that a man must break it with an
ax, although a monkey both picks and opens it easily
—held twenty-two "niggertoes", wedged together
like the segments of an orange.

We went ashore at one of the tiny clearings while
the caboclos were loading wood. The palm-leaf hut
there was raised on four stout palm logs; its wooden
floor was only a foot above the water, which already
was beginning to recede. Animal life here, too, was

strangely absent. During the trip upriver I saw only a few parrots, a band of brown monkeys, and an animal on a sandy beach I believed to be a tapir, but it disappeared so quickly I could not be certain. Mosquitoes, however, were not so shy.

A parana-miri, an arm of the river which comes back to the main stream again, was choked with beds of purple-flowering aquatic plants and rank-growing arums; mangroves were common. Once on shore, the jungle wall separated, trees stood out as individuals —figs, hardwoods, silk cotton, rubber, ceiba; miriti palms grew in dense clumps, the slender assais in groups of four or five. The miriti provides the Indian with material for his house, fiber for his hammock, food for his family; the assai supplies his drink.

I was greatly interested in the assai. The Duke had told me the favorite drink of the Paraense, assahy, was made from the purple fruits of this palm. The reddish-purple refresco is drunk with mandioca. Quinine is added often as a malaria preventative. The Paraenses like assahy so well they have a little couplet:

Quem vai para Pará para; (Whoever goes to Pará stops;)
Quem toma assahy fica. (Whoever drinks assahy remains.)

Looking at the assai palms and remembering the little couplet made me think of what a good time I'd had in three-hundred-year-old Belém, or Pará, as the jungle city usually is called. Sophisticated capital of the state of Pará—its Grande Hotel, Theatro da Paz, Government palaces, comfortable homes, electric trams, and tree-lined boulevards as modern as those in other large South American cities—it is still a part of the jungle, existing for and off its products.

We stayed in Belém nearly a week. Senhor da Silva interviewed and hired a crew, cook, and three caboclos—mixed Indian breeds, to run his large sturdy launch, the *Itaúba,* up the Amazon. Thus we were assured of good accommodations and probably better men than we could have hired in Santarem.

While the Senhor and my husband were busy, I rested in our comfortable room in the Grande Hotel, or explored the city.

A quarter of an hour from the Praca da Republica, the beautiful central park, with its tiny tables under age-old mango trees, I found myself beyond civilization. The noise of crowds and traffic was stilled in the depth of dark tropical jungle; here tall creeper-laden giants fought upward and stretched orchid-bejeweled arms to the sun.

Belém, city of nearly 300,000 inhabitants, must wage relentless war against an ever-encroaching tide of tropical vegetation. Already—since the collapse of Brazil's rubber boom—the jungle has reclaimed miles of suburban land developments. Three or four weeks without attention and a picada or road, often a mere tunnel with walls and ceiling of living green, is impassable for traffic. Wide streets, lined with mellow-colored houses—orange, blue, pink—soon become grassy lanes; ferns, vines, grasses, weeds grow defiantly between cobblestones, in the crevices of mosaic pavements and roof tiles, and moss and lichens cling wherever they can find a foothold.

To realize fully just how easily the jungle can overthrow a city, one has only to see the ruined cities of Yucatan, Guatemala, Peru; the massive stones of pyramid and of palace relentlessly pried apart by the growing root. Walls that were built to stand for centuries crumble and fall when the jungle attacks.

"Great wreckers," the Duke used to say. "What a leverage!"

Someday, if Belém should relax her vigilance, the jungle may take advantage of the city's long siesta—from eleven to two—to attack from three sides, to close in on Belém and push her off the land into the river.

I had learned something from my first grass hut experience. Grandmother's silver and little clock, my pottery, even my beloved negligees and Russian boots —what the Duke called fripperies—were in storage or packed in our city apartment. Breeches and boots, for the field; comfortable wide-legged trousers or slacks of denim or khaki, for other occasions. But I went feminine on underwear; after all, I still was a woman. Cold cream, powder, and other make-up I consider essentials; they do as much for the morale as medicines do for the body.

Once my outfit was ready—the Duke bought snake serums, quinine, sedatives, morphine, and other medicines—I spent most of my time at the Doco do Vero-pezo, the See-the-weight Dock, where the boat basin is packed with sailing ships, their lateen sails of solid blue, red, saffron, pink, or brown. The early morning sun glinted on picturesque boats, laden with jungle treasures. Men, nearly nude, unloaded on the quay balls of "black gold"—crude rubber—splitting it open to see if they had been cheated by stones placed in the center to increase its weight—a trick of wild-rubber gatherers. Other gangs shoveled great heaps of castanhas or Brazil nuts—"niggertoes" we call them; cacoa was another common product.

The public market back of the dock was beautiful to see and to smell with its mounds of golden, green, purple, and cherry-red fruits; as well as delicacies and rareties unknown in northern climates—maracajú, cupuassú, of applelike taste, mamão or papaya, and dozens of others. The air was heavy with heady, exotic perfume, compound of citrus rind, of pulp of custard apple, of fragrant ground jungle bark with which every mulatto girl powders her hair, as an irresistible aphrodisiac. Its scent penetrated even over and above that of the fish market. There I saw pirarucú, the "cod" of the Amazon—fat, reddish-brown, the largest strictly freshwater fish in existence, reaching a length of eight feet and weighing from sixty to one hundred pounds, its scales nearly two inches wide. We carried bales of this dried, foul-smelling fish up the Tapajoz; it is the meat, the beef of Amazonia, even as mandioca is the bread. The Duke bought tins of butter for our table; the pilot and caboclos preferred that made from turtle eggs, rich in fat.

I was glad, when at last I saw the *Itaúba*, that we were to travel on it, instead of taking the *Belém* or another of the big twin-screw triple-deck boats of the Amazon River Steam Navigation Company. They are comfortable, clean, and specially designed for tropical life, with fine wire screens replacing wood, wherever privacy is not essential; this insures free circulation of air with adequate mosquito protection. Space is provided for your hammock on the flat upper deck; the majority of passengers, many of them pajama-clad, spend most of their nights there, as well as their days. I was amused when I discovered that although the food—served at long tables on the open second deck—of its kind is excellent, passengers so plebeian as to wash must provide their own soap and towels. We could have made better time on a river steamer, of course, but there is something homelike about having your own boat.

The *Itaúba* sailed at dawn for the Rio Tapajoz.

Belém is not situated on the Amazon, but on the Pará River. The Amazon proper now has no delta like that of our Mississippi. The water at its mouth is deep and the silt it carries down is washed out to

Left: A common method of building native houses on a hillside is to step them up in terraces. *Right:* An unusual view of the beach, Rio de Janeiro.

Cattleyas and other orchids of the jungle. Hundreds of rare species are to be found in Brazil and, to a lesser extent, in other South American countries.

sea. The Amazon delta once extended about three hundred miles into the blue Atlantic, but the ocean has eaten it away. The main channel of the great river is dangerous, because of the gigantic bore or wave, which, sometimes thirty feet in height, travels at express-train speed and destroys everything in its path. Its roar can be heard for miles. For this reason few boats dare to enter the Amazon through its main channel; traffic is by way of Belém.

Soon after leaving the dock we passed a small native river boat, a gaiola or "bird cage", its decks heaped with bags, baskets, and casks.

Late in the afternoon, we put in at a small ranch house on the Island of Marajo, where we met Ramondo. After leaving the island, with its forests of buriti and assai palms, we steamed slowly along, tying up for the night at a small wood station where the crew worked hour after hour carrying sticks on their shoulders, from shore to boat. Some of the launches burn coal, but it is very expensive.

Hours later we entered a deep, natural channel, the Breves Strait; the Amazon is connected with the Pará estuary, which is very wide, by a number of these narrow canals, some only a hundred feet wide. So winding was the strait that the exit seemed choked with vegetation and I wondered how the launch could proceed. But always we slid around a bend and the way lay open before us.

It was still. There was no earth but only two walls of liana-draped giants standing with their feet in the

clear water; waves from our boat surged against their
trunks and spread, with widening ripples, into the
matted undergrowth. There were no birds, no animals, no reptiles, no life of any kind. Twice we saw
tiny huts built on stilts above the river, but they were
closed and deserted. Once we passed a dugout, but its
Indian occupant swept by without a glance and vanished silently around the bend.

When we entered the main stream I could almost
believe that old historians told the truth and that
Pinzon really did sail twenty leagues up the Amazon
before he discovered he had left the ocean and filled
his casks from a "sweet water sea." For we had entered an inland sea, a world of water without bounds.
O Rio Mar, the River Sea, say the Brazilians proudly.
If it were part of my country, I'd be proud, too! The
world's greatest river—nearly 4,000 miles in length—
it spews into the ocean from its yawning mouth 240,-
000,000 cubic feet of muddy water every minute,
staining the blue Atlantic yellow for almost 600
miles. The world's greatest river island, Marajo—
larger than Portugal, twice as large in area as Massa-
chusetts—lies like "an egg in the jaws of a dragon"
in the estuary of the Amazon.

Even the Duke, who had worked on the Madeira,
was familiar with Manaos—nine hundred miles from
Belém, on the Rio Negro—and other cities and towns
along the river, was impressed anew. Always quiet, he
now talked even less.

The *Itaúba* plowed its way stoically up the great

stream. Sometimes, I thought, we would never get to
Santarem. We passed it in the night and the pilot
turned into the blue Tapajoz without danger as the
river was high.

The red-headed giant walked intently toward me. I
backed away, as far as I could go. Behind me the
bank of the Cuparí, a tributary of the Tapajoz,
dropped steeply to the water. My second grass hut,
built by Mandurucu Indians, was a day's paddle
downstream. With an effort I held my voice steady.

"You're the only red-headed man around here,
aren't you?" It was so obvious, but I couldn't think
of anything else to say.

He acted as though he had not heard me. "What
are you doing here?"

"Looking for orchids."

"Orchids! Well, there are plenty of them here—
miles of them. What are you going to do with them?"

"Paint them. Maybe someday I'll put them in a
book. Come down to our camp and I'll show you my
drawings."

He said nothing; I decided it might be as well to
keep quiet, too.

Finally he roused himself. "I'll show you orchids:
Cattleya aclandiae, pale green with lip of purple;
Cattleya crispa—a blossom white as snow, marked
with glowing ruby; *Zygopetalum maxillare*—how'd
you like to see that—with a purple ruff on its disk,

shaped like a horse's hoof? Ay, lass! Let's get going.
And don't run away, either. I could crush you just
like that." He scooped up a small butterfly and closed
his hand, then opened it to show me brilliant,
crumpled wings, slim legs that stirred feebly, then lay
still.

"Mad as a hatter," I thought, wishing I'd stayed
home where I belonged instead of going orchid hunting with Ramondo and two caboclos. The Duke was
to be gone a week or more, making rough maps of the
country. He had taken the launch as far as Itaituba,
below the rapids of the Tapajoz; from there they
would work slowly downstream. The Tapajoz is one
of the main waterways from Cuyabá, in Matto
Grosso, to Santarem, all boats having to portage
around the falls, of course—one of the waterfalls,
Salto Grande, is more than thirty feet high. I stayed
at the hut. The Duke wanted to finish the job quickly
and he could do it more easily without me. Anyway,
I'd had enough jungle and to spare in the last few
weeks—I could do with a week's rest. Not that there
wasn't plenty to do around the hut, for the ants ate
everything in sight. I had to wage a constant war to
save enough clothes to enter civilization again.

But the orchids were so plentiful, Ramondo said,
so near at hand. He brought in a few blooms and *this*
was the result. What would he think when he returned to the boat and found me gone? I opened my
mouth to call to the giant to stop, then closed it.
What could I call him? "Hey" didn't apply and it

seemed silly to yell "Mister" at a rough, red-bearded man, skin burned to a rich mahogany, whose only garment was a pair of tattered cotton trousers held up by a piece of string. Clop, clop, went his heavy leather boots. I choked back an hysterical giggle. I should have been terribly frightened. But I could not resist the lure of a red-headed Scotchman in the jungle, who tossed out botanical Latin offhand.

Caramba! Red-headed men have always gotten me into trouble. First it was the Minister, then my cousin who left me roosting on the bell in the church steeple, then my uncle, who encouraged my tomboyish acts (so Mother said) by letting me sit beside him around the campfire while on moonlight nights the hounds gave tongue as they chased some wily fox across the mountain. And now this!

The Cuparí valley is deep and narrow; the air is always warm and moist, even in the dry season. We were following a little path, such as wild animals might use at night, deeper and deeper into the jungle. I might not be really scared, but I certainly was uneasy. Soon it would be dark.

Suddenly the path bent sharply. It came out upon the bank of a broad, calm stream; we merely had taken a short cut to another bend of the river. A large hut, conical, built of bamboo framework clinked with mud, roofed with thatch, was built beneath a spreading mango tree. On the sandy beach before it stood a woman—young and lovely, with a bright red girdle of some soft cloth twisted around her waist;

her breasts were full and firm, her stomach flat. Two babies tumbled on the ground, a third played happily in the water. I caught my breath; the woman was a Mandurucu, that I knew—her hair long and black as a raven's wing—but she had two red-headed babies!

Amazonia is full of tales of men, white men, gone native. You hear about them in every little jungle town, in every South American bar; you meet them in queer, out-of-the-way corners and in the lobbies of down-at-heels hotels. But where or when had I met a character such as this?

The Scot said nothing but strode into the hut. I didn't know what to do, so I followed him in. It was very dark. I hesitated, for there was an unusual odor in the air, a scent I had not met before, a heavy cloying scent that filled my nostrils and drugged my senses. The man stirred a fire burning upon the primitive hearth until the hut was lighted well. Then I saw them. . . .

Huge, velvety cattleyas, smaller, more dainty laelias—pink, rose, lilac, purple, yellow, gleaming snowy-white ones—thousands upon thousands of exotic blooms. From top to bottom they lined the walls, they hung on lianas from the thatch, they lay in great heaps upon the floor. In some the crisp petals were bruised and torn, others wilted on the hard-packed earth, still others were fresh and moist as though just wrenched from their support in some hidden, orchid-haunted glade.

I stared in amazement. Orchid perfume seemed to

swirl around my head. With roars of laughter the giant filled my arms with blossoms, blossoms worth a fortune figured by Park Avenue standards, blossoms worth almost their weight in gold. He hung a chain of white orchids round my neck, he put pale-gold orchids in my hair and dropped others—green, lilac, bronze—at my feet.

"Take these, and these, and these!" He tore the delicate blossoms from their stems, his huge hairy hands crushed their beauty even as he had crushed life from the gay butterfly. "Now you can paint. . . ."

I stumbled into the air, really frightened, almost sickened by the heat, the perfume, the excitement. Roars of laughter, wild, mad laughter, followed me, peal upon peal. The woman hurried past me to the hut. "Wait! Wait!" she said quickly as she passed. Inside I heard her voice, firm, soothing, caressing, scolding. Gradually the laughter ceased. He answered a word or two, in a tongue I could not understand. Softly she commanded; like a child he obeyed.

She came to the door and beckoned. I went to her. "See," she said, "he sleeps." He lay upon a woven mat among the orchids. Gently the bronze-colored hands took the fragile flowers from my arms; gently she dropped them on the pile upon the floor. "Tomorrow fresh ones; fresh ones wet with dew. My man," her voice was proud, "my man he know."

Under the trees the dark shut down like the snuffing out of a light in a windowless room. I could not go to the boat now. I must wait until morning. And Ramondo, what would he do?

I sat down outside the door to wait. The Scotchman taught her English, of course, I thought, listening as she bathed the little ones and put them to sleep in hammocks. Later, she brought me a bowl of stew —fish, hearts of palm, and peppers—hot and steaming. "I go get men," she said and, before I could stop her, disappeared in the direction of the river. How did she know where to go?

The fire died down; only embers, dull, glowing, remained—embers and the heavy scent of dying orchids. Outside it was so black I couldn't see my hand a foot before my eyes—a black wall that shut in the hut, the Scotchman, the orchids, and me.

"Ay lass! Be there?" he muttered, half awake. Thinking he was calling the woman, I answered, saying she had gone to get Ramondo at the river.

He stumbled to the door, stepped through and sat beside me. The silence of death reigned in the clearing—there were no night noises, no hunting animals, no croaking frogs, no fiddling insects—just silence.

My hands were clammy; perspiration matted my hair and dampened my cotton shirt. And then the strangeness passed, it seemed somehow natural I should be there, and we talked.

Who was I? Where was my husband? What did he do? Where were we going, and when?

He talked like a man starved for the language of his kind, but my questions he pretended not to hear.

Of orchids he talked freely . . . his interest only in the bulbs. He used to send shipments regularly to England, France, and Germany.

"It's dangerous, hard, the life I live." Through the dark I heard him sigh, a patient sigh that expressed something of his feeling about the heat, the fevers, the poor food, the snakes, the wild Indians.

"Why don't you go home?" The question was asked before I thought.

No answer. He stirred uneasily. There was no sign of the woman or Ramondo.

"Don't you miss the cities?" Fool, I said to myself, but I could not seem to control my tongue.

A long silence. "Not any more," he said finally, but there was no bond between us now. We sat there in the blackness, with a queer strained feeling between us. Goose-pimples chased up and down my arms.

He rose, went into the hut, fumbled around for a few minutes and returned. He carried something—what, I could not see.

Suddenly a queer wailing noise swirled out into the jungle night—squeaks, trills, almost sobbing notes. My hair crinkled—I could feel it. I am certain it stood straight out from my head, for I was alone in the jungle with a madman and a bagpipe. I knew about bagpipes. Uncle was musical, too! I clenched my hands to keep them from shaking. The music changed to a lower key . . .

"Sing, damn you!" he shouted suddenly. "Sing . . .
sing . . . Eat, drink, and *sing,*" he misquoted, "for
tomorrow we die!"

I can't sing. I never could. My parents spent a great
deal of money on my musical education, unfortunately. I can play the piano, a little, but not
enough to count. I worked out a scheme, at six or
seven, to help with the practice. Scales can be run
easily with one hand. They don't interfere at all with
the reading of a good book.

But I sang. I don't know how many songs, either.
I started with "Yankee Doodle," the first one I
thought of, and sang it through to the tune of
heavens-knows-what. When I'd stop to take breath
he'd bellow "Sing!" and off we'd go. We ran through
all the songs I knew and started on hymns. "Nearer
My God to Thee," rolled out over the black night to
the accompaniment of a stirring martial tune; "Rock
of Ages" called forth a mournful dirge. Hoarse,
quavering, my voice only a croak, I obediently re-
sponded to "Sing . . . damn you . . . Sing!" with
renewed efforts.

Finally my voice was almost gone—only a hoarse
guttural sound rewarded my efforts. "Sing!" he said
threateningly. So I gasped on and on. Louder and
louder he played; wilder and wilder was the music.

A faint gray showed in the east when the woman
returned with Ramondo. She had lost her way. Natives do *not* have any special sense of direction.

We spent three days with the red-headed giant and his woman. Madman though he was, he knew more about orchids than any other person I have met.

Southeast of the Rio Cuparí there lies a virgin field of orchids—orchids that will bring rare reward to their collector. There I breathed their fragrance and saw their colors—purple, white, crimson, rose, lilac and gold—their exquisite fragile beauty gleaming among the treetops, on rocks, on branches reaching to the sun along the banks of tiny streams, on the trunks of strange trees, but always on live trees, never on dead ones. They seemed so delicate, resting there, like butterflies, or "ghosts of butterflies."

While we sat beneath some orchid-laden tree the Scotchman told me stories of the orchid's love life, of how, standing at the highest point of plant evolution, they must trick and trap, by every means conceivable, the insect visitors without whose help they cannot propagate.

"Their perfume—jasmine, lily-of-the-valley, tuberose, vanilla, rose—even the foul, evil breath of the stanhopea," said he, "is to attract butterflies, beetles, and flies; remember—the stench of carrion may mean a wealth of orchids, magnificent in their beauty."

"Ugh!" I shuddered. "Don't mention carrion and orchids together."

"Haven't you ever seen any butterflies?" he asked cryptically. "Beauty and foulness often go hand in hand."

I had no answer. Only the week before I had passed

a swollen, bloated, dead alligator, left by the receding waters high on the shore; fat, white maggots crawled in and out of rotted flesh, nearly hidden beneath a cloud of red and black and crimson wings—gossamer wings that quivered, that trembled in the sunlight as a flock of butterflies drank greedily of the poisonous, exuded liquid. That was so horrible I couldn't bear to think of it.

Listening to him, following him, crawling through reeking, miasmic bogs, attacked by swarms of ants that poured out from their nesting place when we pulled the plants from the trees, always hunting some rarer, more choice bloom, I began to feel a little mad myself. Orchids began to look to me uncanny, as though perhaps they did bring death and destruction to the robbers who snatch them from their humid homes. Among the natives, superstitions—chiefly of ghost spirits, of blood, of disaster—haunt orchids wherever they are found.

In Petén the natives will not touch, even for a day's pay—untold wealth to them—the tall, lush spikes of a crimson epidendrum. "Blood from victims of Cortez," say they. But the "Holy Ghost" orchid is sacred to the brown men of Panama; to them idolatry, paganism and Christianity, are so mixed that "the Dove"—shielded within pure waxy white petals, with head, beak, throat, and outspread wings—really symbolizes the heavenly dove that descended upon the Son of Man.

Yet orchids are not parasites—they ask nothing but

support from the trees to which they cling; their
food stored in bulbs, taken from the air and the rain,
they are self-supporting, as much so as any iris or
lily that grows. But all orchids are not epiphytes, or
tree perchers; some of them are terrestrial. I saw both
kinds here; I saw orchids only a quarter of an inch in
diameter—tiny, golden-brown, pansy-faced—and
the cattleyas, eight or nine inches wide. Their very
names—Bee, Bird's Nest, Spider, Viper's Jaw, Hooded
Dwarf, Tiger—indicate how closely orchids imitate
other forms, solely to assist them in fertilization.

"No living creature," said Orchid Jamie, "even
woman, the loveliest of women, is so decked with
beauty, or so wantonly offers herself . . . color, perfume, form. . . . See," his great square-tipped finger
touched ever so delicately the vivid scarlet lip of a
snow-white Cattleya.

"This is the insects' landing field. Watch." At that
moment a small hawkmoth, its tightly curled proboscis like fern fronds in the spring, lit on the cinnabar-
orange lip of a comparettia. Unrolling its proboscis
the insect plunged it down into the two-inch nectar-
filled spur of the orchid, while its head burrowed into
the pollinated anthers of the orange flower.

"Now he'll pay for his sup of honey," said Orchid
Jamie. The moth fluttered away, his head dusty with
the precious seed, and lit upon the wider platform
invitingly provided by a large golden comparettia.

"Perhaps a new variety was born there," Orchid
Jamie remarked quietly. "Is it not a miracle of evolu-

tion that the male stamens in these same blossoms will not be ripened 'til the female has withered?"

"Ever see an orchid seed?" He plucked a ripe pod from a tall, leathery-leaved plant clinging tightly to a fig tree. "Look!" A fine, dustlike powder showed faintly in the crushed pod. "One orchid may produce 180,000 of these minute seeds," he said gravely, "but only one may live. Even in a greenhouse it may take as much as seven years, after the seed has sprouted, to produce a blooming plant. And it may be a considerable time after fertilization before the seed takes hold and sprouts."

Few people know that the vanilla vine is an orchid, a terrestrial orchid, which has evolved into a liana bearing as many as forty beanlike pods a year. Its delicate, pale-green and white blossoms are not large, but their perfume permeates the jungle for half a league about.

Mad Orchid Jamie. He shared his rich knowledge generously with me. I brought from the jungle much that was to remain with me always and, I must confess, many things that I struggled to get rid of promptly!

The Duke had not returned when I reached home with my orchid booty. The hut was cool and comfortable after the heat on the river. I lay down in the hammock. I had a little fever and no desire to have another attack such as I had suffered in Matto Grosso.

We were more than one hundred and twenty-five miles from Santarem and a doctor. Late that afternoon one of the Duke's crew paddled, in a hired dugout, into camp. "The Senhor Boss will not return for yet another week," he told Ramondo.

My housekeeping duties were light. The hut was like Orchid Jamie's, only not so large. Our tables,

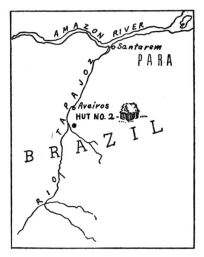

stools, and the long bench outdoors, where I worked in good weather (we had a few hard showers), were made of palm. We brought with us the Dutch oven and varied our diet of fish, beans, farinha, and rice with an occasional roast fowl. Game was very scarce. We shot monkeys for the men—they were very fond of this meat.

Mandurucus visited us nearly every day. They brought small presents of fish, monkeys, and once an opossum which was delicious when roasted. These Indians are very friendly to the Brazilians. Early in the nineteenth century they warred upon the settlements, but soon the two races united against a common enemy, the Muras Indians, and the truce still holds.

I painted and took notes, waged many a battle with ants, and photographed all the lovely tropical scenery around the hut. I tied a string around the camera lever and took my own picture; none of these last pictures will appear in any book.

But I went less and less seldom on long walks. Shortly after I returned from my orchid treasure hunt, I noticed a sore-feeling lump on the back of my thigh, so situated I could not see it even with the aid of my mirror, but had, alas, to sit upon it. I hesitated to speak of this to Ramondo. But now the sore lump had become a huge, abscesslike swelling, and I limped up and down the earthen floor of the hut in agony. I could not bear to walk about; nor could I stand the torture lying down. At last I had to tell Ramondo.

"I get," he beamed in his calm manner and hurried out. Thinking he meant to bring herbs for a poultice, a favorite Indian remedy for everything from snakebite to boils, I settled down to wait. The hours passed. Frantic, I walked back and forth. Days passed. Three of them. I lay on the ground and beat it with my fists. The caboclos withdrew to a safe distance and left me alone.

End of the third day. A short, plump figure stalked

in the door, walked over to where I lay, weeping, on the ground, grunted a phrase or two to Ramondo, who picked me up and placed me face down on the blanket. A hasty examination, a swipe over the skin with some cool-feeling paste, a wait of a minute or so, two sharp, stinging cuts, and the fat loathsome grubs incubating incognito beneath my skin were squeezed out. Berne flies or what not—I remembered the warning of the kind father from Missiones—they did a grand job.

The old Indian woman cleaned the wound, smeared on a cooling paste of herbs mixed with monkey grease, and dropped a blanket over me. Worn out, I slept the clock around. When I awoke, she was gone. The only pay she wanted was a handful of fishhooks and a string of bright-green beads.

After this experience I became an inventor. I propped up a large mirror on the table, tied a string to the small one, and moved it up and down behind me; by becoming a contortionist I could see all parts of my anatomy and managed to remove quite a few unwelcome guests. With all my care, however, I carried a number of immigrants illegally into the States and surgical aid was needed to remove them. They are now saved to posterity, reposing in alcohol in a hospital laboratory.

The next time I saw the old Mandurucu woman she was bending above her garden in a tiny native

village of half a dozen cone-roofed huts. It was a little
village out of Paradise, a tiny Eden on the Rio Cuparí,
a narrow, deep-flowing, satiny stream that feeds the
Tapajoz.

The jungle here was singularly beautiful, great
ferns, vines of vanilla orchids spraying over the tops
of the branches and cascading down over the little
thatched roofs. The village sloped to a silvery beach
and was mirrored in the clear, dark-blue water.

Each house had a garden. Each garden was fenced
off with split palm, to keep out the horde of strange
pets and naked brown babies running freely about.
A baby peccary rooted at the gate, atop which
perched a black howler monkey and his buff-colored
mate. A flock of curassows, big, orange-billed, turkey-
like birds, scratched and cheeped in the clearing. A
baby tapir sunned itself before the old woman's door.

I pushed open the gate and stepped into the garden.
In spite of all the difference in time and place, the old
woman there reminded me irresistibly of my grandmother—the turn of her hand as she tended a plant,
the loving pat to a mound of earth. Her round, wrin-
kled face beamed up at me. Delighted at my visit,
she showed me about her garden. Assai palms, a little
later in the year laden with thirty-pound bunches
of purple fruits, waved overhead. Humming birds,
brilliant green and blue, hovered over morning-
glories, orchids, and trumpet vines of orange and
scarlet; elephant-eared plants—leaves dappled with

gray, white, yellow, orange, and scarlet, grew in rich profusion.

Although I spoke not a word of the native Esperanto, Lingoa geral, we conversed, literally, in the language of flowers. The old Cuparí herb woman was not only a truly skilled native doctor, she was a naturalist. But, after all, although I recognized in her garden many plants of which I knew the Latin names and she did supply me with their Indian equivalents, she would identify no new plants for me. She volunteered no new information.

Still it was with reluctance that I tore myself away; stepping over the sweet potato vines and through the walls of sugar cane. I crossed the clearing where the women were making the glazed pottery for which the Cuparí is known, sat down in my waiting montaria, a dugout of the yellow stonewood tree, the itaúba, and turned my back on that lovely peaceful village.

At the junction of the Cunarí with the Tapajoz, I just missed seeing an interesting fight between an alligator and what the caboclos insisted was a water boa, an anaconda. The two reptiles, apparently locked in a death grip, churned the water to foam, but neither of them came again to the surface. I was disappointed. Furthermore, some of my ideas regarding life on the Amazon had been shattered; nowhere had I seen the amount of game I had expected. The

game is there, so are the snakes and the birds, but they
are hidden away in the depth of the jungle and few
of them may be seen without careful search.

The Duke was home when I arrived. For once he
looked somewhat at a loss. And well he might. The
hut and all it contained was a mess; no other word
describes it. Someone, something, had broken in the
carefully barricaded door and wrecked practically
everything in the place. Bats had taken possession of
the roof and foraging ants, tauoca, had eaten everything in sight. Even the Duke's favorite trousers,
spilled from the metal trunk, had not escaped.

He held them up to the light. "Isn't there a place
where they repair these things?" He looked worried.

"Repair them?" They looked like a sieve. "You
could take the band and have new pants sewed on,
I suppose." He didn't think it funny and continued
to fuss while the caboclos tried to restore order.

I didn't ask him about the job. I knew by his
expression he was afraid the cost of building the camp
would be too high for Senhor da Silva. The profit in
wild crude rubber is so small.

For days the Duke and his men explored the field,
investigating the courses of the tributaries of the
Tapijoz and charting the streams roughly with the aid
of a Brunson pocket transit, in order to prepare a
preliminary map of the region. He made notes, also,
on the topography adjacent to the streams and covered the area between them. Each night, notes taken
during the day were plotted on the skeleton map.

A tentative camp site, near the river and on fairly high ground, was chosen and located.

To secure a fair approximation of the amount of wild rubber in a given area, the Duke made actual count of the number of trees on a small typical tract; this number is used as an average stand to compute the entire region.

Henry Ford now controls 3,000,000 acres of jungle land on the banks of the Tapajoz, an ideal location for a rubber plantation. He has not as yet, I understand, taken out any amount of rubber.

We had just gone to bed, our hammock ropes well smeared with balsam to keep the fire ants away, when a great commotion broke out among the caboclos. The Duke went out at once armed with gun and flashlight. He found them greatly upset. With Ramondo's help, order was restored, but all vowed they were leaving in the morning. The place, they said, was infested with evil spirits—could not the Senhor Boss hear them?

Listening carefully, the Senhor Boss heard them. Cries, moans, came from the direction of a near-by clearing. Ramondo, the Duke, and I took the medicine kit and went to investigate. It sounded as though someone were seriously injured and in great pain.

A crude, hastily erected hut stood beside a tiny brook; no hut had been there the previous week. A fire burned before it. A dozen or more Indians, wild and savage-looking, lay or sat before the fire; there were only two women among them. The groans came from within the shelter. The Duke made as though to enter, but they shook their heads violently, motioning me to step inside alone. The Duke and Ramondo, handing me the medicine kit, sat down by the fire to wait.

On the mat lay an Indian, tossing from side to side. His eyes were rolled far back in his head, so that only the whites showed. Froth bubbled from one corner of his mouth. He certainly did look like a very sick man. I touched his hand; it was icy cold.

The Indians, crowding into the hut behind me, talked together in low guttural tones, then tapped impatiently on the kit I carried. Ramondo had spoken to them in the Lingoa geral; if they understood they refused to answer. But they were thoroughly familiar with the white man's habit of dispensing medicines to the natives.

Having no medical experience of any kind, I was worried. If I gave him a pill and he died—well, that would be hard luck for me. I would surely be blamed. If he died anyway, I would be blamed for that, too.

I opened the kit, mixed a husky dose of bicarbonate of soda and dissolved in it three quinine capsules. It certainly would not hurt him; it might help. Two of the Indians held his head and slowly we poured it down him. Then, after a little while, I gave him a sedative to make him sleep.

While waiting for the sedative to take effect, I kept my finger on his pulse; his hand was warmer, the pulse steady and strong. Soon he stopped tossing and seemed to be in a deep sleep. The foam no longer trickled from his mouth. I covered him with his mat and in so doing looked closely at his features; he showed distinct Negroid characteristics, as did the other natives.

All night I watched beside him. He woke early the next morning, hale and hearty, so far as I could tell. I stepped outdoors, then halted in amazement. Stepping from a thicket was a buxom young woman, in her arms a tiny babe, wrapped in a blanket. She entered the hut and all the Indians again crowded inside.

The Duke and Ramondo laughed and laughed. I didn't. "Couvade," the Duke gasped between chuckles.

Couvade it was. I had heard of the practice before; the father goes to bed while the mother gives birth to the child. For nearly three weeks the husky Indian stayed in bed, tended with loving care by his wife and the other natives. He ate the choicest morsels, drank the native brews, and otherwise enjoyed himself. The wife and the little new baby received no attention of any kind. She washed, gathered fruits, fished, and in fact did nearly all the hard work.

We found out nothing about them except that they were on their way up the Cuparí, having come from near the falls of the Madeira, about four hundred and fifty miles up that stream. Otherwise they refused to answer questions. They begged beads and fishhooks; in return they gave us fresh fish and fruits.

The woman fell in love with my sole remaining piece of underwear. I gave it to her. It almost required the service of a shoehorn to get her into it. A funnier sight I never saw than that short bronze figure clad only in a pair of pink silk scanties.

Chapter Twelve

PATAGONIA: GONE WITH THE WIND

*Third grass hut—Buenos Aires—The snake's hips—
Tall tales—Comodoro—Santa Cruz—Valley of the
Rio Chico—Guanaco's graveyards—The joke on
Drake and Magellan*

OUR BUSH SHELTER, my third grass hut, was built
beside the Rio Chico, in a valley where seed-bearing
grasses grew. A muddy marsh, a pantano, dotted with
pools of deep clear water visible only in daylight,
showed bright-green along the river's edge. It was
January, but summer in Patagonia.

The hut, the size of a small tent and the shape of
an Indian tepee, was made of brown pampas grass
laid over a frame of poles dragged from the river
valleys; its floor was soft deep-piled guanaco skins,
buff and brown; its walls also were covered with the
wind-breaking pelts. Shut into our fur-lined nest,
even with a cold, steady wind outside, we were comfortable. It was the typical hut of the sheepherder
of the pampa, better made, more expensive hides;

there was no window and the hide door was tied tightly from inside after we had entered. The whole house was strapped down to earth by thongs of guanaco hide passed completely over the hut and tied to stakes driven deep into the ground; without these our Patagonian home would have blown completely away.

We were situated in a valley at the turn of the river, where high barren bluffs broke the force of the wind that swept relentlessly down from the snowy Cordilleras. Our closest contact with real civilization was Santa Cruz, an important port on the Atlantic Ocean, about one hundred and eighty miles southeast of our camp. An occasional estancia—sheep or cattle ranch—could be found in some of the more

fertile valleys; the houses in these ranged from mud
huts to real homes, with moderate comforts.

Our bedding rolls served as saddle blankets by day;
laid on the skin floor of the hut at night, they made
a comfortable, warm bed. Our bolsterlike saddles
we turned into pillows. Some of the nights were very
cold, so cold that we used heavy guanaco-skin robes
as covers.

A few yards beyond our hut was the cook tent,
down wind; it was really a lean-to built of brush
and skins. We were sheltered by the guanaco and we
ate guanaco. It tastes to me like young kid. We also
ate quantities of mutton; neither the Duke nor I
have eaten mutton since. Most of our meat was
cooked asado, that is, roasted in the hide. We had no
vegetables except dried beans and rice; I drank tea,
coffee, or boiled water—the others preferred maté,
which to me is bitter and disagreeable to taste. Occasionally we varied our diet with a goose or duck, but
after a heavy windstorm the sand made all food taste
alike.

One night in January I slipped out of bed and
looked outside; the stillness seemed uncanny after the
unending howl of the pampero that had blown steadily for days. Around the embers of a little fire the
gauchos slept, heads covered with their blankets; the
Duke had left three men to guard me. Some guard,
I thought in amusement. Had Matéo been with us,
he would have slept across the doorway. But Matéo
was far away in Matto Grosso, or else in Asuncion

with his three women, whom he beat every day. I was
very tired and went back to bed. I had ridden miles
over the bare, wind-swept pampa, racing ostriches
and guanacos, trying to sketch and fill in the time
until my husband returned to camp. But tired as I
was, I couldn't sleep. I counted sheep, in Patagonia

there is little else but millions of sheep, but to no avail.
So I gave up and began to review all the interesting
things that had happened on this trip.

An acquaintance of the Duke's, Señor Eduardo
Gomez, had invited him to go on a search through
lower Patagonia for cheap land which, by irrigation,
could be made into profitable sheep country, land that
could be made to provide more than a bare sustenance
for large flocks. Work was scarce in the States. No

other opening having presented itself for a few
months, the Duke was anxious to accept, even though
Señor Gomez' offer carried with it small compensa-
tion. But my husband's interest was aroused, particularly as he already had made a railroad reconnaissance
in Patagonia, and was disappointed at the outcome of
his other railroad job in the Argentine, on which he
had promised employment to Matéo. I knew, too,
that he wanted to visit again the land he called the
"kingdom of the winds."

I was the fly in the ointment.

"Most esteemed Friend," wrote Señor Gomez.
"Deeply as it grieves me, I must decline myself the
great pleasure of your company. Patagonia is no place
for a woman. It is a man's land; woman has no place
in it, except on the estancias and in the towns; and
seldom there. To take a wife on such a trip as this!
No, no, my Friend. But if you decide to come alone,
I will welcome you with open arms. My house is
yours."

"Go alone," said I to the Duke. "See if I care." But
I did care and he knew it.

"I'll take you as far as Comodoro Rivadavia," he
promised. "That will give you an idea of the country;
then you can go back to Buenos Aires and wait for
me." That was the way it was settled.

Modern and patently prosperous as it may be,
"B.A." is not an impressive sight when approached
by the muddy waterway of La Plata, the Silver River.
Sebastian Cabot, the Venetian navigator, sailed up the

Paraná and supposedly continued until almost in sight
of present-day Asuncion; silver plates and ornaments given him by natives caused him to believe the
country rich in silver mines, thus the river's name.
A clean, white city, a Hispanic Chicago, Buenos Aires
lay low on the horizon as we glided into the shallow,
muddy estuary, so wide it was more like a sea than
a river.

"Greatest port in South America," said the Duke.
"This city really is indebted to engineering. Formerly
the pampero used to blow the water right out of the
stream, leaving the city stranded. The land you see
now was nothing but an unsanitary mud flat, twenty
or thirty feet above high water."

"What's a pampero?" I broke in.

"You'll learn soon enough. Engineers dredged out
the silted bottoms, drained the swamps, built up the
entire waterfront with sea walls, esplanades, docks—
in short, a beautiful modern city."

I was so busy after that I forgot to ask more about
the pampero; I found out about it later, when it
blew not only the cook tent but the cook into the
Rio Chico. I had time, however, although we were
there only a day and a night, to notice that Buenos
Aires has the biggest, handsomest men in South
America (they look conceited), with the most elegant deep-crowned fawn-colored hats and the most
superbly fitting trousers—the snake's hips—and that
they spoke a distinctly different Spanish idiom in
"B.A." Also that the women had deep unctuous voices

and bosoms, and after thirty a seductive shadow of down upon the upper lip.

"B.A." also has the most delightful milk wagons, like giant toys, painted freshly in primrose yellow, rose, turquoise, and decorated with wreaths and scrolls of flowers. And the subway—the only subway in South America—is, like the king's daughter, "all glorious within"; the entrances are handsome in Spanish tiles, bright in color and design, while the manners of the guards and passengers are quite as conspicuously in contrast to those of North America.

The only other impressions of the city I remember are enormous numbers of terutero birds hopping around on spindly legs in private gardens; they utter shrill cries if a stranger approaches, especially at night, and are thus prized as "watchmen."

The Mihanovitch Line boat was small but not uncomfortable; even so, I was glad when we anchored in the roadstead off Comodoro Rivadavia. For a change, the sea was not high; often a ship has to wait three or four days for the water to become calm enough to land passengers. There is no harbor. The government has built a long steel jetty, where their boats dock, but other craft are not allowed to use it. A concrete breakwater was started, but never completed. Steep, bare cliffs rise six hundred feet or more directly behind the houses, tanks, and oil derricks on the narrow strip of beach. There is no vegetation, no trees, no grass, no flowers, nothing but sand and wind.

It was then late November, but my impression of
the climate was completely obliterated by the wind,
the terrible Patagonian wind which blows from the
Cordilleras and often, for days at a time, makes it
impossible to walk upright; one must proceed by
crawling undignifiedly on hands and knees.

Tall tales of this wind are told in Patagonia. A
soldier, practicing at target shooting, was killed by
the bullet from his gun flying back and piercing his
heart; a lady preparing a fowl for the pot was saved
the trouble of picking it by the wind, which stripped
all feathers from the bird—it blew them into a pillow
case and all she had to do to make a new pillow was
to sew up the end; a poor widow, with no skin cover
for her bed, was, by the grace of God, made a present
of one at no cost to herself—a young guanaco, trying
to buck the wind, had all its fur stripped away, the
force of the pampero so tangling the fleece there was
no need to have it woven into a coverlet.

We spent a night at the Hotel Colon, where Señor
Gomez had promised to meet the Duke. There we
were given a message to come down to Santa Cruz.
I decided to go along, perhaps go down to Punta
Arenas, then return with the boat to "B.A."

The little I saw of Comodoro through the dust
gave me only a vague impression of it; a half-dozen
hotels, of which the Colon, with baths, and bedrooms
opening onto an open patio, with a few flowers in
tubs sitting around here and there, is the best. The
town is divided into squares; most of the miserable

Upper: Fish traps such as these are common along the coast of Brazil. *Lower:* All the products of the jungles are brought to Para's waterfront markets.

Upper: The solid wood wheels of carts such as this may be seen in many Latin American countries, especially Chile, Brazil and the Argentine. *Lower:* Llamas, relatives of the camel, are commonly seen on the high Bolivian plateau, while the llama's ancestor, the guanaco, inhabits the pampas of Patagonia.

houses and commercial buildings are of corrugated
iron, with an occasional structure of concrete. There
are a few stores; one or two large ones sell everything
from sewing machines to peanut butter.

Our boat entered the junction of the Santa Cruz
and Chico rivers at high noon, when the tide was
running out. Santa Cruz is a small town built on a
level strip along the estuary. Like others along the
Patagonian coast, it has no plaza; no one ever walks
the streets for pleasure. The houses are of wood or
clay, with mud floors, roofed with corrugated iron
which is heavy enough to withstand the ordinary
wind. The pampa here is nearly flat, with a range of
blue hills rising in the northwest.

Señor Gomez met the boat. He was tall, stout, and
pompous, high hat held under his chin with a strap;
his gloves, riding whip, and boots would have graced
the bridle paths in Central Park.

I packed in a hurry, transferred my things to shore,
and by three o'clock we were on our way—five men,
Señor Gomez, the Duke, and I. The Señor led the
way, I followed, and the Duke rode behind me. Our
men, with the extra horses and pack animals, which
must be changed every day, strung out in a long row.
The bell mares, madrinas, kept the horses bunched
together fairly well; they are never ridden and their
troop stays close beside them at night. Although we
were traveling light, with our extra clothing, toilet
articles, and medicines in our saddle bags, we had
three troops of horses, twenty-four in all.

"Why do we have so many horses?" I asked Señor Gomez, riding up beside him.

"Too dangerous with only one mount each. One of them might step in a hole and break a leg, or get saddle sores, or run away. This is no country to be left afoot. Look at it."

The ground was bare, stony, not a bush, a blade of grass to be seen; for miles around Santa Cruz everything but the earth itself had been burned as fuel. The horses' hoofs left no marks on the soil; a few ruts marked the trail. Later, even the ruts disappeared and I still believe the Indian trackers in Patagonia are gifted with second sight.

I dropped back to my place and we rode on. We must have been a strange procession. All of us wore heavy sheepskin-lined coats with the high collars turned up to keep out the wind. I had thick woolen underwear beneath my woolen riding breeches and a flannel shirt under my windbreaker. I was nearly as broad as long. But every time I looked up and saw Señor Gomez, I felt like laughing. He still wore his high hat; the Duke and I had caps with ear flaps.

The first day's ride and camp were new and interesting. We slept in the open. Rolled up in blankets, I enjoyed lying beside the small fire where the cook roasted an armadillo in its shell for dinner. One of the men caught it easily as it scampered over the brown grass; these little animals, curious survival of a bygone age, are nearly blind in the daytime. Unlike our northern armadillo, it did not curl up in its shell, but dug its four little feet so deep into the ground that it could hardly be pried loose. In soft soil, explained the cook, seeing my interest, they sink their armored plates so deep that one must dig beneath them to dislodge the armadillo.

Day after day we followed an almost invisible road across the camp, as the pampa is called; sometimes we followed the old Indian trail, a branch of which runs from Santa Cruz to join the main trail along the Cordilleras. Occasionally we stopped for supplies at a sheep ranch, usually run by a Scotchman, but more often we ate fowl killed near a water hole, or a stringy rhea, the South American ostrich. Once we found a fresh ostrich egg and made an enormous omelette, which was rather strong tasting, but a welcome change from so much meat.

Except around the water holes, game was not very plentiful; at least, not as plentiful as I had expected to find it. Pumas, hares—two kinds, the real hare and another species peculiar to the pampa—armadillos, and guanacos were most often seen.

Near the Sierra Ventana, almost in its shadow it appeared, I saw a small band of guanacos. The guanaco is the New World camel, the ancestor of both llama and alpaca. Today it is extraordinarily timid because the Indians and settlers in Patagonia have hunted it so remorselessly for its skin and its flesh. The cloaks of the natives are made from the tanned hides of these animals, the hide worn outside, often painted in bright colors and elaborate designs; the

fur is worn next the bare skin and is incredibly light
and warm, a characteristic of the camel tribe.

Guanacos are small, only about four feet tall, but
endowed with great speed and endurance. Their backs
are arched, with little or no tapering at the waist;
their faces are round, short-snouted. They swim like
ducks, when cornered or when they desire to cross
a river. Sometimes, when we passed lagoons or pools
and even along the river banks, we came upon numerous skeletons of guanacos which had either starved
to death during the preceding winter or, if superstition is based on fact, had made their way there to die.
This story of the guanacos' graveyard is common all
over Patagonia. It apparently has no more basis than
the one commonly told of the elephants' graveyard in
Africa.

We crossed a high yellow pampa, where mirages
followed us along the horizon. The wind blew steadily, except when we dropped down into the barrancas,
some of them more than a hundred feet deep. I was
glad when we reached the valley of the Chico and
made permanent camp. After the barren pampa, it
seemed like a meadow at home. Señor Gomez liked
this valley. He and the Duke were gone days at a time,
investigating the possibilities of the surrounding country. I sketched, painted, and, for the first time in
all my travels, worked hard to keep from being bored.
At night I lay awake and listened to the wind chuckling, roaring, shaking the frail hut until I expected it
to fall upon my head. I dared not think what it must

be, at such times, beyond the shelter of the bluffs. If
it slackened at sundown, it began again the next
morning at nine. Often now we had hard rains, last-
ing for two or three days.

The country is interesting, if one can stand the
cold, the howling wind, the cutting feel of the eternal
sand against one's face. But Patagonia seemed to me
unreal. Always, all through its turbulent history,
strange stories of its inhabitants, its animals, its plants,
have been told. Drake and Magellan found immense
footprints in the sand and, although they never saw
the Tehuelche Indians, decided that if they really had
such large feet—say twenty-four shoe—they must be
at least ten feet tall; thus the giants of Patagonia.
It appears that the mild Tehuelches put one over on
Magellan when they faked this formidable-looking
spoor.

I don't really like Patagonia. The saying of the
Patagonians about calafate berries is not true in my
case; I have eaten them, but I shall never go back.

"You would come," said the Duke when I complained about the bleak, cold country.

"Make a better choice next time," I retorted.

Chapter Thirteen

JAGUAR HUNT IN THE CHACO

*Matéo and Poco-mas return—Grass hut number four
—The Inca's treasure—The caravan trail—I become
an engineer—The Gran Chaco—Grass hut number
five—Vampire legend—The jaguar hunt—Hummingbirds in Green Hell—Matéo's death—Green
Nandurie—Break camp*

WE WERE IN Chile, enjoying a busman's holiday,
when the Duke received word regarding a job in the
Gran Chaco of Bolivia, the great wilderness which
I longed to see. Some of the work would take us up
in the foothills of the Andes; the balance would be
in the Chaco proper.

Matéo met us at Santa Cruz de la Sierra, having
ridden from Puerto Suarez, on the Paraguay, across
the Chaco to Santa Cruz, a distance of at least five
hundred miles. Onça was as fresh as though he had
only crossed the river. Matéo beamed all over his great
fat face. I was glad to see him. My joy was short-lived.
He had such a surprise for me, he said, and produced

Dom Poco-mas like a magician pulling a bunny from his hat. However, he always had been allowed to choose his men; the Duke did not interfere.

We followed the caravan road to within a few miles of Samaipata, and built our stone hut, hut number four, on the rolling slopes where they lift steeply to the skirts of the Andes. Here we would escape the hordes of snakes, of fleas, flies, spiders, mosquitoes, piums, flies so tiny they look like black pepper drifting through the air, toads and frogs as large as bunnies, that live and multiply by dozens in the lowlands.

This hut, too, was a product of the country. Flat, irregular stones, precariously piled, or so they appeared, were laid to a height of some six feet; in reality these huts often stand for centuries. The house was about eight by ten, with a very thick grass thatch, probably eighteen inches thick, laid over a gabled frame of poles and weighted down by stones. A beaten earth floor sufficed here, for it was dry and cold. No windows, a blanket hung before the door, two folding camp chairs, a folding table, hinged down the middle, made us very elegant. We had folding cots and blankets for bedding. I felt quite Abercrombie-Fitchie!

Our hut was the admiration of all the natives, who came to stand and stare in at the door (especially while we ate). It was also the envy of a large boa, who took up his residence in the roof and lived off the field mice and insects which lived there too. For this reason Matéo refused to allow the snake to be killed, although I had visions of finding it twined around my neck some morning, or of stepping on it in the dark.

The cook stove was a rustic one of stones, to match the house. A few hours ride into the lowlands furnished us with good food—yellow potatoes, fresh beans, beets, and plenty of game and fowl; ducks were plentiful, but I pined for thick, juicy steaks and other things, such as celery, lettuce, greens, that were not obtainable. One night, after I had complained bitterly about the food, Matéo joyfully brought to me a large bowl full of chalona soup, the chief staple of the high plateau region. I ate it and ceased to complain ever after, not knowing but what he might find some more of it in his house-to-house canvass for choice delicacies for our table. Chalona is "jerked" mutton—mummified meat, in other words; it is dried in the sun and wind until it is little more than hard, brown strings. It tastes like nothing else on earth; once tasted, it is never forgotten. Boiled plantains, too, become tiresome, but after I sampled a mess of fat white grubs, rolled in egg and fried in palm fat,

I decided to eat only beans and rice and game. Matéo said the grubs came from trees and were very clean. But, somehow, the thought of them . . .

I rode with Matéo upon the high plateau at about 10,000 feet elevation. There, many of the houses were built of tapial—wet earth mixed with chopped grass, then stamped into long wooden molds; the bricks looked like adobe. The roofs were of thatch supported by poles dragged from the distant lowland valleys.

Near us were some barren rocks known as El

Fuerte. Here, Matéo said, Yupanqui, the Inca emperor, built his fortress so that from it he might wage war upon and conquer the tribes of the great wilderness below. "Tunnels under the rocks," he said, "are filled with gold, carven images of beauty and value, and emeralds and other precious stones." While we were there it was rumored that a mummy had been found with jeweled ornaments; the countryside is so impregnated with ore that the mummy had been well preserved.

Just before we finished this section of the job (in jungle country it is easier to cover the work in sections), and were ready to leave for the Chaco, the Duke stopped me as I was about to start off with my paints. "There's an error in the south line," said he. "The distances don't come together. I'll have to recheck."

"Anything I can do?" I asked, somewhat surprised. My husband seldom talked about that part of his work, although he never took a job without consulting my preferences.

"I thought perhaps you'd act as rodman this afternoon," he answered. "Matéo and the crew are hurrying to clear the underbrush, so that tomorrow I can set up the transit and measure the angle and distance to the last point."

"What do I have to do?"

"All you have to do is hold the rod on different stations—stakes driven in the ground at various points —so I can check the distances between them," he explained patiently. "We can do this rapidly by stadia."

"What on earth is stadia?" I asked, interested at the idea of really working at engineering.

"Stadia is measuring distances with the transit instead of the chain Matéo uses. Stadia is faster, but not as accurate."

"Is that all there is to engineering?"

"Well, not quite. You'll see. Get your horse and come on."

The south side was not covered by such dense growth as other parts of the tract. I went from stake to stake, holding the leveling rod at an exact perpendicular on each one; the Duke followed, taking his readings with the transit. He explained that the space on the rod intercepted between the two horizontal hairs in the transit is the distance between the stake and the transit, if multiplied by one hundred.

We found the error between the fourth and fifth stations. I decided not to become an engineer. It requires too much multiplication.

Much has been written and sung of the Argentine pampas, of their limitless rolling stretches, their gauchos, their music, but although the name Chaco during the past few years has been impressed upon the minds of North Americans, little is known of that region.

The Gran Chaco—the great wilderness lying in the

fork between the Paraguay and Pilcomayo Rivers—
has always been, and still is, a land of mystery. Its
natives, some twenty tribes—claimed by historians
to be descendants of, or to have been controlled by,
the Incas—are a law unto themselves. Their language,
writes one of the good Jesuit Fathers, is like "the
sound of ducks quacking in a pond rather than the
voices of men talking." He declares they "hiss with
their tongues, snore with their nostrils, grind with
their teeth, and gurgle with their throats." The birds
of the Chaco, its animals, even its reptiles, appear
different from those of other lands, although their
ancestry may be the same. Even the trees, the palms,
are different from those growing just across the Paraguay. Not a stone is found in all that great wilderness.
This is the land over which Bolivia and Paraguay
fought the bloody war ended in June, 1935, by a
treaty of peace signed by their foreign ministers in
Buenos Aires.

Paraguay won, at least to the extent that Bolivia
still has no worth-while seaport of her own. She has
the use of Arica, Mollendo and Antofagasta on the
west coast; she owns a mudbank, Puerto Suarez, on
the Paraguay opposite the Brazilian city of Corumbá
—this port is worthless during the dry season and,
even in floodtime, the river there is too shallow to
accommodate large vessels. Bolivia is too large, too
rich, to stay forever bottled up.

The Chaco proper is much larger than the disputed
territory. It extends from the Argentine marshes of

Santiago del Estero to the plains of Chiquitos in Bolivia and from the Rio Paraguay to the mountains of Santa Cruz de la Sierra and Tucuman.

Late one afternoon we crossed the Rio Grande, the swift black stream below Santa Cruz; the ford was low, the banks of the river deep in mud. Even so, the current carried us far downstream before we reached the opposite shore. We camped that night beneath the stars in the Gran Chaco.

For two days we followed the sandy yellow caravan trail that runs, between thicks walls of matted forest, for five hundred miles from Santa Cruz to Puerto Suarez on the Paraguay. Matéo talked with our Indians, then decided to head south, straight into the heart of Green Hell. This is the name by which the Chaco has always been known in South America. In the rainy season much of the Chaco is flooded, but now in August we rode endless miles with not even a pool at which we could water the horses. It may be thirty or forty miles between water holes. Fish lay gasping in mud puddles—the stench sometimes was almost unbearable. But this course brought us within easy riding of the stretch the Duke had promised to survey for a ranch owner.

For over a week we fought our way through the marshes, the wooded islands of palm trees, and thorny shrubs. We were now close to the country of the Tobas, the fiercest, the most savage of all the Chaco tribes. They live in the swamps along the Pilcomayo and are said to raid caravans on the Santa Cruz trail and to rob and kill ranchers in or about the big marsh.

Two or three times, as we rode, with a peculiar feeling of watchful eyes upon us, we saw nude brown bodies slipping easily between the thorn trees, but they never molested us in any way. "Leave their women alone, they no bother," Matéo said gruffly when I questioned him fearfully about them.

"Watch Poco-mas," I warned, but that brave engineer showed no inclination to wander.

We camped on a grassy plain dotted with carandai fan palms. The country is deceitful; always it seemed as though a ranch, a homestead, should be just around the next clump of trees. But there never is—the plains, the swamps stretch on and on, their inhabitants wild creatures, both human and animal.

Esparto grass, thick and spiny, grew three or more feet high around the cactus clumps; the latter had spines six inches long. Some of the cacti were so tall they reached nearly to the tops of the palm trees—approximately forty feet. The spiky frills of wild pineapples showed between tufts of grass; these the Brazilians call gravatas. They give virgin country a distinct character of its own; some perch high on trees, but many are scattered on the ground, green rosettes of fleshy leaves being visible from a long distance.

Gray secretary birds stalked sedately among the trees; "Shoot-and-be-damned," they appeared to say, with defiant brushlike tails stuck stiffly outright. Tiny birds, I do not know their names, chased each other through the bushes. Flights of ducks whirred over-head; ibis, flamingoes, and herons watched from a safe distance.

A few poles, grass, and a palm thatch—in less than a day this time my fifth grass hut was ready. We were camped now in the great wilderness of the Chaco, more than a hundred miles from Santa Cruz, with nothing near us but jungle. This hut was like the rough "retiros" of the herdsmen, who often do not see the main ranch house for weeks or even months at a time, living, eating, sleeping in the wilds. Once we had decided on the site, the men set to with their machetes, mowing off brush, slapping it against the sapling framework, shearing off sheaves of bright-green grass, and packing the fragrant bales into the brush. The sheaves of grass were bound to the frame work with tough lianas. My house looked like a pretty green basket, both inside and out and, although it was only a temporary shelter, I was very proud of it. But its looks belied its comforts; inside it felt like one of the old-fashioned hay-insulated fireless cookers. As a great concession, Matéo had stretched a heavy blanket before the door, but it provided me with little privacy; closed, the toldo (the Guaraní word for house) was so close I could not get my breath. Insects of all kinds settled in clouds on any exposed portion of the body. I slept in head net, gloves, and clothes, under a mosquito net; I nearly roasted alive. The Duke, being of sterner stock, refused to make any concessions other than the usual precaution of crawling under a net to sleep. That night he accidentally pushed up against his mosquito bar; when he awoke the next morning his entire hip looked as though it had been peppered with buckshot.

Long before dawn next day I heard the men stirring, smelled the persuasive odor of broiling duck, on its palm grid over the fire, and the pungent, burnt odor of freshly roasted coffee. I turned over for a nap. Presently I heard the smack of saddles being slapped on horses' backs and could stand it no longer. I stuck my head out of the door to see what was going on.

"Tiger hunt," Matéo said briefly. "Want to come?"

Did I want to go!

While my horse was being saddled I gulped down a cup of coffee, then announced I was ready. Matéo scowled ferociously because I had eaten no breakfast. He looked at the Duke with obvious disapproval of his lax ways with a woman.

I looked with disapproval at the horse he had saddled; a more mouselike creature I never did see. But after a few miles of thorn thickets, matted lianas, pools where hungry piranhas lay in wait for any prey, I applauded his choice.

We took no dogs, although they are generally used in hunting the big cats. We had two, but, like the majority of canines in this region, they had been gelded and were absolutely spiritless, and no good for hunting, or anything else. I do not know why the Paraguayans and Brazilians geld their dogs.

Upper: Hut with trimmed thatch and reed walls. *Lower:* The jaguar is the most beautiful of all the jungle beasts. It is hunted, usually with dogs, for its spotted pelt.

Upper Left: South American swamps closely resemble those of tropical North America, being filled with the same lush growth of water plants and reeds. *Upper Right:* Yungas of Bolivia. *Lower:* Natives threshing on the high plateau.

Lacking good animals, Matéo decided to beat the game from its covert, although it is a dangerous, hazardous method. The Indians agreed somewhat sulkily to spread out and, when a tiger was located, surround the thicket or swamp in which it took refuge and drive it towards the hunters by shouts and drumming.

Our five Indians were mounted on good little ponies. They were equipped with spears, crude drums —hide stretched over hollow logs and my aluminum kettles; alas! they were never seen again. Every man was voluminously diapered with loose folds of cloth, and wore fringed leather aprons and leather leggings. Machetes at their belts, long-roweled spurs on their horny bare heels, they were almost impervious to the spiny scrub of the Chaco.

But I was not!

We all used the Argentine saddles, recaos (ricados, really)—two bolsters over which a sheepskin is thrown. They are more comfortable than the hard, curved troughlike saddles used so much in South America, both to ride and to sleep on.

The mosquitoes were bad, but the almost invisible piums were worse. They filtered through my head net into my eyes, my ears; if I opened my mouth they flew down my throat. I had the terrible thought that they might not all die—suppose they began to hatch! Not a nice idea.

Riding beside me, the Duke slapped viciously right and left. "These damn mosquitoes," he growled, "would certainly kill anyone in short order. An ani-

mal, tied here for a night, would never last until
morning. They will even kill a calf in a corral." Red
grasshoppers, as large as humming birds, flew up under the horses' feet.

We splashed through the edge of a long, narrow
lagoon; the jacaré (yacaré, in the Chaco) lay boldly
and indolently along its banks like logs in a boom.
Following the mud-baked shores, we rounded a bend
and witnessed a jungle drama which haunted my
dreams for weeks.

In the shallows a red cow fed hungrily on the lush
aquatic growth; the Chaco is filled with thousands
of wild cattle. Suddenly, without warning, piranhas
attacked, bit off her teats; the blood flowed so swiftly
that the weakened, maddened animal became confused and plunged deeper into the water instead of
turning toward the shore. It was all over so quickly—
I watched, horrified, sick—it seemed only a second,
in reality a few minutes, until the cow's head disappeared in a froth of fin-beaten, gory water. We
went on. Her mooing seemed still to echo in our ears.

"It will always be there," said Matéo. "Remember
the cries you heard in the upper Paraguay? A batalão
capsized there years ago; you can still hear them
screaming."

Matéo and our two camaradas told many tales of
the Chaco as we rode—of Yace Yacere, the gnome
of the forest, and his pranks; he rides through the
air on Urubú the vulture and steals children from
beside their sleeping parents. They told of vampires;

tales as grisly as any that ever came out of medieval
Europe. I walked my horse carefully around the
clumps of thorny thickets and listened, while icy
prickles ran up and down my spine, to the story of
Yandarai as it came in swift, gutteral snatches, picked
up and translated into English for us by Matéo.

An Indian's mother, who was a very old woman
of at least forty and, so the son thought, a witch,
was jealous of his young wife and hated her. She was
his only woman—he was young then—and he loved
her. He never struck her, never made her carry a
heavy burden. This made his mother very angry. But
one day his wife sickened and died. He feared at first
his mother had poisoned her. It was night when she
died and he saw her breath drawn out from her as a
whirlpool sucks down a butterfly.

He knew then it must be the vampire of the marsh,
who flew at night low over the toldos where the
dying lay and seized upon their souls; it had come
to claim the soul of his wife. He was sick at heart.
He begged his mother, now that she had her wish
and his wife was dead, to save her soul from the vampire—to work some magic charm upon her.

To this his mother agreed. For several days she
boiled herbs and burned aromatic grasses. She kept
this up day and night, although she herself began to
be ill and failing. On the third night she fell asleep
in the toldo. When she woke in the morning she was
like a different person. She was young again, she was
lovely; her eyes were bright, her lips were crimson.

her hair glossy black once more. She sang happily as she prepared yerba maté and took it to her son. But he shrank from her in horror; she was now the image of his beloved wife, who had died.

There was no doubt about it; she had not been trying to save his lovely young wife at all. She herself had taken the soul from the vampire of the marsh. What could he do? If he killed his mother, as was his first thought, he would drive the soul of his wife out of her resting place and back into the clutches of the vampire. He knew, too, that the vampire would exact some pay, some toll of blood, in return.

Within the week his cattle drooped, sickened, died off like flies. He tried to stay awake at night to watch; as certain as he slept, he woke in the morning faint, ill from loss of blood. But his mother-wife bloomed, and grew plumper and plumper. She did not care that his cattle and even he himself were the price paid for her return to youth.

But one night he woke at midnight. He rushed to the door of the toldo just in time to see a great swarm of vampire bats, hundreds and hundreds, drift on silent wings out of the jungle and fasten upon his cattle. He grabbed flaming torches from the fire and drove them off, then herded the cattle across the river, while his mother-wife screamed and screamed in the toldo. He paid no heed. But when he returned at daybreak only her limp body, drained of blood, lifeless, was there to greet him. The vampire bats, cheated of their prey, had turned on the woman and claimed their pay—taken back not only the soul but the blood as well.

The Lenguas, a Chaco tribe, break the bones of their dead so that they cannot return as vampires.

The Chaco Indians are simple souls who prefer infanticide to abortions and do not consider bumping the grandmothers off until they are at least forty.

At daybreak we rode past a settlement—wattled huts made of saplings thatched with marsh grass—and saw an old man drinking his chicha, fermented honey from wild bee trees, out of a human skull. Small, stingless bees crawled over our clothing.

We left the bank of the lagoon; the horses sank deep into the swamp muck. Wild pigs grunted, rooting, before us—peccaries, and a domesticated-looking creature, big and fat, that reminded me of home. A little further on we met an Indian boy herding a half-

dozen large rooters; he overtook a great sow, heavy
with young, and sprang upon her back. I watched
in sympathy and some trepidation. There flashed back
to me a picture of a small, skinny person with hair
black and shiny as the little Indian's own, riding a
pedigreed sow round and round a farmyard in New
York State, till the sow dropped dead from exhaus-
tion.

The Indians, who were leading, halted. Ahead lay
a circular patch of dense jungle; on the wet mud
at its edge were round, deep cups, fresh jaguar tracks;
water still glimmered in the depressions. I moved
back and waited, a hundred feet or more from the
side where the three hunters stood, their Winchesters
ready. One of them had hunted before with Matéo.
He belonged to a great family of jaguar hunters in
Minas Gereas and was as famous in his state as Sacha
Siemel is in Matto Grosso. His last name is Junqueira
—his first name I never knew. Matéo called him Com-
rade. Only his friendship for Matéo caused him to
subject himself to the indignity of hunting without
dogs.

Then began such a din as surely never was heard
before. I held my hands over my aching ears. Gingerly the riders closed in, leaving only the side toward
the hunters open.

Above the din I heard Matéo yell. Following his
pointing finger I saw the great spotted cat crouched,
snarling, on a limb, directly over the head of one of
the Indians. Engrossed, watching the thicket before

him, the Indian forced his horse farther into the
matted jungle growth, paying no heed to the warning
cries. Apparently he thought them only a part of the
hunt.

The tiger was in a fury. Frightened, at bay, it kept
up a steady growl like the rasp of a rusty buzz saw.
How *could* the Indian help but hear it? Against the
dark-green foliage of a wild fig tree the jaguar's beautiful coat shone with burnished luster, brown spots
on pale gold; I could not, from where I sat, see his
light-colored stomach. Tail swishing from side to
side, the huge male, larger, heavier-boned than a
cougar, gathered his muscles to spring.

Matéo, hesitating no longer, shot once, twice, as
he galloped swiftly up. The cat dropped like a sack
of meal through the branches and struck the ground
with a dull thud.

"Close to three hundred and fifty pounds," the
Duke exulted. The meat was for the men; the hide
for me.

It was almost sundown when we neared camp. We
rode back almost in silence, all of us busy with our
thoughts. Never have I seen the Gran Chaco so
beautiful.

There are fewer flowers in the jungles of Green
Hell than in Amazonia. But if eighty of the four
hundred species of humming birds are Brazilian, at
least a hundred, I should think, must belong to the
Chaco. We passed a marsh filled with lilies, red, orange,
yellow. A humming that lacked the whine of gauzy

insect wings rose from the swamp. The blooms were literally swarming with tiny, darting, iridescent bodies flashing in the sun. The blur of beating wings gave an unreal shimmer of light to this lovely fantasy.

I have not said much about the humming birds of South America, where the exquisite and entrancing thimblefuls of warm flesh and jeweled feathers are so varied, so prolific. But though the gardens, the wilderness of Brazil, shelters more humming birds than any other region on the entire continent, it was, strangely, in Green Hell that I saw the loveliest.

As soon as work in the Chaco was completed, a matter of three days, we returned to our camp on the slopes of the Andes. The Duke was anxious to finish his report and start for home.

The trip was so long, so hard, that I was worn out and decided I would stay quietly in camp for a few days. It was extremely comfortable there. The climate at that altitude, something between four and five thousand feet above sea level, was cool and delightful; a breeze blows almost continually over the marshes below. Deflected upward by the rising ground, it sweeps up the serried steeps, drives across the cold barren plateau ten thousand feet above sea level, and whistles at a hundred miles an hour through the uncounted snow-sheathed peaks of the distant Cordilleras.

It was fascinating to think of this and to look up

at the grandeur of the plateau, blue with distance. The Duke went off to the north, to stake out a sheep ranch for an optimistic American, and Matéo, on his Onça, turned to the south, to finish his job. I sketched, rested, and mended our clothing.

The Duke returned early, to my surprise; the sun was just dropping when his sorrel (we had bought him in the Chaco for four dollars and he was as pretty a little pony as ever I saw) came trotting over the ridge behind us. As soon as Matéo returned they could compare notes, make up their final report, and *that* job would be done. The Duke went over his data, going outside now and again to watch for Matéo.

We would have to go ahead and eat supper without him. There was no sign on the lower trail of any rider. I think that the Duke was a little uneasy even then. He said nothing, as usual, but seemed to be on the alert, hearing every sound. I, too, grew restive, fretting, chiefly because Matéo had promised to bring me a thick steak from the ranch for my supper. A sooty, purplish dusk settled over the low lands; the peaks of the Andes were outlined with fire from the setting sun. The glow faded. The after-glow commenced and crept up their sheer flanks. Still no Matéo.

We sat down and picked at the supper Dom Poco-mas set before us. There was hot bean soup, I remember; I remember because I can never forget the smell of that soup. I have never eaten it since.

I had just taken a mouthful when the Duke, who sat facing the door, abruptly pushed back his camp chair. He was outside before I could turn around. I could not see at first in the dark, but a horse whinnied right in front of the door, and by that time I could see the dark bulk of it and the great shapeless mass astride.

"Quick!" The Duke spoke tersely to one of the men. "Bring a light," and to Dom Poco-mas, "Untie that other leg."

Untie that other leg? Matéo was . . . tied on?

The Duke himself was working swiftly at the horse's side and in a moment the great ungainly hulk pitched over into the men's arms; they lifted Matéo's inert body through the door and into the hut. They laid him on the floor. I lifted his head into my lap. The measuring chain was clutched so tightly to his breast that we could hardly take it from him. Matéo was completely unconscious. The Duke felt his pulse at once, rolled back his closed lids.

"Snake bite!" He knew the symptoms well. The Duke examined Matéo swiftly. His swollen, discolored ankle and leg were apparent; in the fleshy part of the ankle were two crisscross cuts from which black blood oozed slowly. They rolled him over and injected the neutralizing serum for unknown snake bite into his back.

"Probably Nandurie," said Poco-mas quietly. "Small snake; see how close the cuts are together?"

My husband shook his head. He could not understand. Matéo always carried with him a snake-bite kit. The Duke felt through the big man's pockets; from his belt he pulled out the outfit he had given him before Matéo set out, for the Chaco is overrun with snakes—large and small. The serum was untouched.

"It tells right here how to use it!" the Duke was stunned. Matéo showed no reaction to the serum. His pulse was rapidly growing fainter. "He could read what to do the moment he was bitten. I *showed* him the directions, in fact, when I gave it to the damn fool!"

"Matéo did not read, Senhor Boss," said Dom Pocomas, shaking his head sadly. "Did you not know that? Always I or someone else read to him your letters and instructions. I thought you really knew. He was very proud, Matéo. He did not want you or the Senhora Boss, or anyone to know."

Yes, he was very proud.

Matéo died in a few moments, in the Duke's arms, without ever opening his eyes. I sat helplessly by, tears running unheeded down my cheeks.

The Duke sat very still. Poco-mas and the men tiptoed softly out. I followed them and left the Duke alone with his friend.

We understood, later, what must have happened. Barefooted always, Matéo had trodden upon the deadly little snake in the dust. He must have known, have felt immediately the effects of that fatal poison even through his vast frame, for he had tied himself

carefully to the saddle and held tightly in his arms
the chain, his Boss's valuable tool. Onça had brought
him home. He had come carefully, slowly, not to lose
or upset his burden, which he sensed was unsteady.

Dom Poco-mas found the next day that Matéo
had been almost five miles away when it happened.
It had probably taken Onça an hour to bring him
back to the door of our hut. He had, undoubtedly,
lost consciousness long before he arrived. His great
vitality and strength evidently withstood the con-
vulsions, which Poco-mas claimed always followed
the bite of this tiny reptile. The men dreaded this
snake, so plentiful in the Chaco, more than any other.
Matéo undoubtedly did not expect to find the Nandurie at so high an altitude.

Poco-mas carried the Duke's report of Matéo's
death to the authorities. We never saw him again.

Matéo was buried at dawn, just under a knoll
on the hillside, looking toward his home across the
lonely marsh. A great mound of stones was piled
over his grave, so that no creature should disturb it.

The Duke was the last to turn away. "Break
camp," he told the men. "I found Matéo's checks on
the southern boundary in his pocket." He showed me
a slip of paper with a row of small even crosses. It
was the only reference he ever made to Matéo's inability to write. His inability to read had cost us too
dear.

Chapter Fourteen

THE DEATH GOD

*Darien jungle—Tales of lost mines—Forbidden coun-
try — Wild Indians — Sloths and coati-mundis—
Chokoi hut, my grass hut number six—The Death
God*

IT WAS TERRIFICALLY hot in the Darien jungle. I sat
in the humid dark and swung my feet over the edge
of the floor of our grass hut number six. We were
camped along the bank of the Chucunaque River
just below the mouth of the Membrillo, a tributary,
near the so-called "closed country" of the wild Kunas
of the hills. Our nearest contact with civilization
was Yavisa, a hundred miles away near the Pacific
Coast.

The Duke, who had cruised mahogany in Santo
Domingo, always had wanted to see the forests of
the Chucunaque and the interior of Darien. Twice
before we had tried to penetrate to the headwaters
of this river and both times we had failed; river
crews are notoriously frightened of this part of

Panama, which has an unenviable reputation as being
death to intruders, black or white. This was the
farthest we had ever been up the Chucunaque.

"You're crazy," the oil man at Garachine, our
first port of call on the eastern shore of San Miguel
Gulf, told us bluntly. "Of course there is timber
there, plenty of it. There is gold in all the rivers,
emeralds have been found, we know there are de-
posits of lead, cinnabar, copper, manganese, and
platinum in some of the rivers' gravels. Panama is
loaded down with rare orchids. But there are nice
long arrows tipped with snake venom, too."

"We'll chance it," I told him, just as anxious to
penetrate Darien as the Duke.

Darien is almost unknown. Only a few white men
have ever penetrated its jungles or its mountains,
which stretch from the Pacific to the Atlantic and
from the Tuyra River to the Atrato Valley—an
unknown land, chiefly unmapped, thousands of
square miles unexplored.

Because of untold hardships, hostile natives for
more than four hundred years have successfully re-
sisted all attempts either to find or to open up anew
the fabled gold mines of Panama—the mines responsible for bringing down upon them the Spaniards and
their ever-remembered cruelties. We know little or
nothing of the tribes who inhabit this vast territory.
Legend relates that in its fastness is a hidden city,
where an unknown, highly civilized tribe lives in

Mayan-like houses in a high-walled town to which there is no road.

I do not believe the jungle conceals another Chichen Itza or a second Uaxactun, although no man can say this is impossible. There would have been no conquest of Mexico if Cortez had not listened to an Aztec's tale of wealth, no discovery of the Pacific by Balboa if he had not believed an Indian's tale of big water to the west. That tribes in the heart of Darien may have a high degree of culture seems to me most probable; I believe that in Panama's jungles lies the answer to many unsolved riddles which archaeologists have pondered in vain. Verrill says the isthmus was inhabited for thousands and thousands of years; its natives reached a high degree of culture long before the Incas, the Aztecs, or the Mayas. Who were these long dead peoples? Pottery, stonework, gold ornaments are found in their graves and, from these records, their history may some day be deciphered.

It is no fable that the Kunas today still send down from their hidden villages, as an annual present to the President of Panama, a bag of gold dust. Nor is it a fable that they still observe the tribal laws against gold—no woman of their race may wear gold ornaments, although silver ones are permitted. No white man may look unharmed upon the rich and abandoned "lost" gold mines of which there are so many rumors; the mines are accursed. Torture and slavery taught a lesson which the Tabasaras of the coast and the Kunas of the hills have never forgotten.

The Duke hired our crew from Yavisa and El Real. The pirogua was small but fast and the Negroes expert rivermen, handling their poles—all travel up river in Darien is by poling—like veterans. They stood out on the flat, overhanging ends of the boat and, aided by the upstream current, fairly shoved the thirty-foot dugout along. An upstream current may sound peculiar, but the tremendous tides flood the Chucunaque and other Panamanian rivers far inland.

The riverbanks seemed absolutely uninhabited; like many of the South American rivers, the natives apparently live along the tributaries. The river was broad, with green grassy slopes dropping to the water's edge; the timber was magnificent—mahogany, cocobolo, cedar—some of the trees rise to more than a hundred feet and are literally ablaze with crimson, yellow, purple, and white air plants, orchids, and lianas.

We traveled slowly, camping each night on a little sandy bar or sleeping in the dugout. There were mosquitoes and sand flies, but not in the numbers we had expected. At the end of the twelfth day we reached the mouth of the Membrillo and camped in a little hollow near by. Our hut was built in the style of the peaceful Chokoi Indians, whose villages we had seen on the Tuira River a few hours poling from Pinogana, a tiny, clean settlement surrounded by cultivated land and orchards of fruit-bearing trees. The Chokoi men go nude except for scarlet breechclouts; the women and children wear little or nothing, usually only a single strip of calico which reaches from the waist to the knees.

Our house was raised on stout poles about nine

feet from the ground; we climbed to it by means of a frail pole ladder and pulled it up for safety at night. The roof was thatch, extending three feet over the sides, the floor of split cane, and in place of the soft bark cloth which the natives use as bedding and floor covering, we put down heavy palm mats and blankets. Our rice, corn, and other food supplies hung from the rafters in baskets or earthen pots. A fire burned slowly on the stone fireplace in one corner of the room.

There was an abundance of game and fish, but we dared not go far from the riverbank. The men flatly refused to do so and we dared not leave them behind as they would desert immediately, leaving us stranded, without boat or food. So this night I was amusing myself by playing the flashlight on a sloth that hung upside down asleep on a branch above me, her baby hugged to her breast. Laziest of beasts, she did not even stir when I flashed the ray directly into her eyes. A little coati-mundi, sleek and pretty, an equatorial edition of our raccoon, was foraging for nuts on the jungle floor. It did not seem at all to resent the light thrown upon it.

I was waiting for an armadillo, which the Duke said would doubtless be abroad at night, as its eyes are suited to the dark. I had not seen one since we left Patagonia; sure enough, I had not long to wait until he came hustling along. This little fellow of Panama actually does roll himself up into a ball inside his carapace. I no sooner flashed my light on him than he curled up, remaining where he was, like an elegant piece of luggage, a round hatbox, perhaps.

It grew cooler; we tied ourselves up in netting and went to sleep.

Things went along very peacefully for a few days. We saw no Indians although the Negroes insisted they were watching us from the forest. The Kunas, relatives of the San Blas Indians of the coast about whom so many stories have been told, are the wild Indians, the dangerous ones; the San Blas have taken the blame, although they are a fairly peaceful tribe asking only to be let alone. Some of their children go to school in Panama and white people are allowed access to their villages, although the government does not encourage such visits, as there have been uprisings, fostered, it is claimed, by abuse of the Indians by white persons. The so-called "white Indians" of Darien are San Blas albinos.

It was the Kunas of whom our Negroes were afraid. They claimed to have seen signs of them and to have found wild turkey feathers stuck in the sand as warning to get out. But nobody bothered me as I followed the Duke through the near-by forest, herding the Negroes ahead of us until they absolutely refused to stir another step.

But one morning I opened my eyes to find the Duke standing at my feet with an expression half-annoyed, half-concerned.

"Look," he said, "we've had visitors." He pointed to the fire before our grass hut. On a little pile of jungle leaves, conspicuously arranged like an offering before an altar, lay a tiny crudely carved image. He picked it up and handed it to me. It was scarcely more than two inches long, made of some dark jungle wood, roughly fashioned, with mere slits for eyes, nose, mouth. It meant nothing to me.

"What is it?" I asked.

"It's an invitation to get out," said the Duke grimly, "and in the famous words of Mr. Dana, 'and be damned quick about it.'"

"To get out!" I exclaimed and, knowing the Duke, "You aren't going to do it, are you?"

"I can't do much without any men," he replied crossly, "and they're all quitting at once. If we don't strike camp we'll be stranded. We'll probably get some poisoned arrows in our backs when we're least expecting it. . . . Roll up that duffle."

Everything that had been unpacked went quickly back into its canvas roll. There were no Indians to be seen around our camp . . . but we could feel their eyes—sharp, hate-filled eyes—peering at us from the jungle.

But I am going back.

Chapter Fifteen

THE LACONDONES POISONED TRAILS

*The cradle—Guatemala—Trip to the coast—The
Professor looked like an angel—I meet the Duke—
A carib dwelling—Jungle serenade—Grass hut num-
ber seven—Lady of the night—Forest primeval—
Cruising mahogany—A ruined city—Hidden village
—Cocks without tongues—Unwilling prisoner—
Ocelots—Escape—Jungle fire—Highway of nations*

THE "CRADLE" LOOKED like the open car of a Coney
Island Ferris wheel. I clutched its side convulsively.
The ropes tightened with a jerk, we swung in mid-
air, rocked a bit, dropped lightly to the deck of the
barge below, bumping gently against the cork mat-
tress protecting the steamer's sides. The aftermath of
a tropical storm sent great breakers thundering on
the sandy, palm-fringed beach of San José, Pacific
gateway to Guatemala.

The tender struck the rusty iron piles of the pier.
In the excitement of getting ashore without falling
into the ocean, I scarcely noticed the huddle of build-

ings along the beach, or the distant cloud-tipped
cones of the volcanoes, dim and mysterious, on the
plateau.

It was time for the train to leave and, in my hurry
to get aboard, I stumbled over ragged porters, beg-
gars, and fishermen who moved lazily along the dingy
water front or snored in the shade of the iron-roofed
buildings. "Familiarity breeds contempt" may be a
cliché, but it is a true one; no longer did I get kinks
in my neck gazing soulfully at a couple of ragged
banana trees or the jagged top of a breadfruit tree
against the sky. It was not that I liked the tropics
less—far from it—but I had now arrived at the point
where I could relax peacefully, without the horrible
fear that I might be missing something of importance.

The first few of the seventy-odd miles of our trip
were not interesting—flat, low country, then gently
rising plains planted with cane, cotton, bananas, and
cocoa. I like to look at cocoa trees; the fruits grow
from the trunks.

I curled up on the hard seat and took a nap. When
I wakened we were well up on the plateau. Pines,
firs—deep, dark-green with immense wide-spreading
tops, reminded me of the Rocky Mountains in the
States; they did not seem, somehow, a part of the
tropics. But we were already in the subtropic zone.
Familiar flowers—roses, violets, petunias—bloomed
around the tiny stations. We crept through a narrow
canyon between towering, cloud-capped peaks and

followed the shores of mountain-rimmed Lake Ama-
titlan; groups of Indian women pursued their endless
washing in the hot springs at the lake's edge.

Guatemala City, five thousand feet in elevation,
centered around its Parque Central, *is* a city; beautiful, mountain-girt, modern, bustling. I cannot de-
scribe it; I was there only a few hours. I left it,
however, with an impression of honking automobiles
and busses; pink, blue, yellow, or white buildings;
tall stone towers of churches, rising above flat red
roofs; an enormous covered market, colorful and
diverting, but not to be compared to the open market
which overflows the street. There gaily dressed natives spread their wares. The aroma of roasting coffee
mingles with the spicy scent of tropical flowers,
copal, the fresh, clean smell of newly wet-down
vegetables; over all hangs the odor of freshly slaugh-
tered meat; armadillos (sometimes roasted in their
shells) and bright-green iguanas are favorite dishes.

This was my first trip on my own—that is, one
for which I personally had made all the arrangements
and taken all the responsibility. All my married life,
it seemed, I had been traveling. But this was different, for the Duke had been very ill with a gastric
ulcer; he was better, out of the hospital, but unable
to work, or to accompany me on this, my first job,
in the tropics. If he became well enough, he would
meet me in Petén, where he had been offered a job

cruising mahogany and other hardwoods for speculative lumber interests.

The trip to the east coast was long and hot. A hard shower in the afternoon, after we had passed Zacapa—where we ate chicken, rice, and red peppers—cooled the air, so I went out and sat on the back platform. The train left the arid, cactus-studded land and entered a humid, moist banana and pine-clad region. The Rio Motagua flowed muddily between mangrove-lined banks, where egrets fished in the shallows or flapped across the stream. In the clearings, palm-thatched bamboo huts tilted at crazy angles, as though unable to hold longer the weight of poverty-stricken, ill-nourished Indians who leaned against them; naked, potbellied urchins ran along beside us, pleading hands outstretched.

Rich Motagua valley; the nearer the coast the more humid it became, the thicker the vegetation. I fanned vigorously and almost, not quite, wished myself back in the States. Flocks of parakeets flew overhead in geeselike formation; parrots screamed; a toucan flapped along after the train like a commuter running after the 8.05. Finally Puerto Barrios—yellow buildings of the steamship company; a mixed population of Indians, Negroes, half-breeds, dogs, pigs, vultures, pelicans—standing in a long row on the old pier; jungle, and more jungle, hemming it in.

The Professor, his pink pate shining in the last light, even without his halo, looked like an angel, waiting there.

He was just as I remembered him, bug bottles and all. No, the nimbus of light and insects was lacking. But, of course, the sun had not yet gone down and his jack lamp was not lit.

"My child," he exclaimed, beaming, as he peered up at me, towering a foot taller than he, "now we will a little chasing together do." He stopped, flushing excruciatingly at the memory his words recalled, the chase of the *Morpho bahiana* at Bahia.

But the chasing we did for the next week was little more dignified than that distracting episode in Brazil. Wriggling on our stomachs through swamps, through tangled undergrowth, soaked in mud, we pursued with infinite patience for hours at a stretch one tiny bug. I have seen the Professor inch himself forward, so slowly that not a blade of grass was moved and within an inch of a swaying boa, perfectly oblivious to the menace of snake or cayman in his absorbed pursuit of a specimen. I have watched him lying in wait to throw his net over a precious butterfly, when one false move probably would have resulted in his losing his head by the snap of an alligator's jaws.

There was a perfect rapport between the Professor and myself; we laughed at the same things, with spontaneous abandon. We both had an eye, or perhaps it would be more accurate to say a nose, for the minute, the infinitesimal, especially the tiny sand flies, small as piums, that swarmed around our heads by the millions.

During the days that followed I blessed the experi-

ence, the training I had received in fine, minute line
drawing from Dr. Robert Dickinson at the New
York Academy of Medicine; medical drawings and
entomological drawings require the same care, the
same steady hand.

The Professor hired a small launch and crew with
which to penetrate the interior of British Honduras
and Guatemala in the hope of securing new specimens. His partner, the Doctor, did the pinning and
preserving of the insects; I did the painting.

The Duke was well again. At least, it appeared so
at that time. "Meet you in Punta Gorda," he wrote.
"It will seem just like old times, our hitting the trail
together." We couldn't know, then, it would be his
last job in the tropics. "No more tropics for you,
ever again," said the doctors.

I was happy as a lark. It was just like starting all
over. Even Punta Gorda—little white houses, picket
fences, palms, hibiscus, oleanders—looked fresh and
clean. Mud, mosquitoes, fishermen's huts, wooden
bungalows back of the neat little town, looked as
though they too had taken on new life.

The *Maya* was due to dock early in the morning.
Long before sunup I was out on the narrow pier.
Two parrots scolded me for disturbing their morning
sleep. I saw the Duke, standing by the schooner's
rail, long before he could distinguish me from the
crowd of blacks that lined the shore; boats are great

events in their daily lives. The Professor had arranged to meet us with the launch at Livingston; we would go down on the first boat out.

The first boat we could get, unfortunately, would be a week, they told us, in coming. "Good chance to break you in easily on a little camp life," said I to the Duke.

Punta Gorda, besides being a clean, attractive town, has an interesting population. The permanent inhabitants are chiefly Caribs, fierce, strong, Negroid-looking natives who originally inhabited the Amazon delta in Brazil and Guiana. Their descendants now are found along the South American coast as far north as Mexico and throughout the West Indies. The men speak one language, the women another. A favorite habit of their ancestors was to raid some peaceful native village and carry off the women; the men were, of course, unable to speak the language of their captives.

By the aid of bribes, near threats, and the promise of liberal portions of "white eye"—the strongest rum in the world, I am certain—we rented a dugout with a crew of three Caribs or "Wykas"—Caribs so like Negroes that we could not have told them apart if it were not for their straight black hair. Further promises of rum induced one of the Caribs to agree to take us to his home locality for a few days, thus giving the Duke a chance to look over the hardwood prospects and me to get in some painting and wild life observation.

The next afternoon we poled and paddled over the mud and sand bars at the entrance of the Rio Grande, north of Punta Gorda. The river was in flood, the current was swift, but we made good time and at dusk turned into a small creek so closed in by jungle that only an Indian would have known

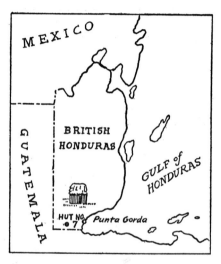

it existed. Hemmed in by green walls, it was nearly dark when we landed on the claybank before the Carib's house. Behind it, I could see a small lagoon like a mirror in the jungle, its banks lost in the evening twilight.

Two small houses, without walls, stood a little way from the main dwelling; we were given our choice of these. It was only a roof of palm leaves supported by four stout poles, from which we slung

our fiber hammocks; it reminded me a little of our
hut in the Chaco, except that there Matéo had built
up the walls, to provide privacy.

Twilight closed down like a purple backdrop.
Monkeys tuned up for their nightly serenade. Tiny
owls flitted across the clearing in search of their supper. The west was a sheet of palest gold. Close to the
creek bank a white egret waded, searching for un-
wary prey; mangrove swallows, white rumps plainly
visible in the half-light, darted back and forth
through the overhanging loops of vines that draped
the trees.

Despite the birds that fluttered, cried, and
squawked about us, it seemed quiet and peaceful
there in the jungle—we two together again. Gray
dusk settled down. Fireflies danced to and fro busily
in the thickets. Birds called sleepily to each other,
then darted to their nests. Herons, kingfishers, parrots, swifts, flock after flock—the jungle seemed
filled with the noise of their wings.

Mosquitoes came, too, with the twilight. Pedro,
the cook, built a smudge fire before the hut. Even
so, we ate our supper of beans, broiled iguana steaks,
rice, and thick black coffee, with our head nets on;
every time we lifted the net to take a bite, at least
a dozen bloodthirsty fiends fought for the honor of
getting the first bite. We crawled gratefully into our
hammocks as soon as we had eaten. Utterly exhausted,
we slept.

The lagoon in back of the Carib house led into a small stream that eventually found its way into another lagoon, larger than the first. Here we made a primitive camp, a leaf shelter as protection from the rain. Dense jungle came down to the water's edge; to the south towered fantastically turreted mountain ranges destitute of life.

It was nearly dark.

Pedro cut an armful of giant canes, forced them upright into the soft ground in the shape of a three-sided lean-to; then he cut strong poles and spaced them evenly, a foot or so apart among the canes, lacing them together, in and out, with lianas and strips of bark. Huge leaves, of palms and other gigantic jungle plants, he plaited together for roofing, laying sticks and branches across it to hold the roof in place. Our hammocks he slung from the stout poles; the earthen floor was covered with woven palm mats. Baggage was piled along two sides, an upended box holding flashlights and our few toilet articles. Our seventh hut was ready and we moved in. It was my last hut, too, for never again did my husband and I camp together alone in the jungle. We were about twenty-five miles northwest of Punta Gorda.

Watching Pedro set the dinner table, palm mat, aluminum cups and plates, ten-cent-store silver, I thought with longing of my first home in Matto Grosso. As the fire blazed up, lighting the jungle clearing, I could almost see, in the leaping flames, another hut, another room—a warm, safe, comfortable room; I could hear the ticking of grandmother's little clock, hear the clink of silver as Matéo, fat and brown, laid the table for dinner; I could see the pottery and smell the fragrance of orchids wet with jungle dew. My first home was gone forever; it was now the haunt of snake, of bat, taken back by the jungle from which it came. Matéo, too, was gone. But the present, my seventh hut, remained. I answered the Duke's hail from the lagoon and walked across the clearing to meet him.

Down the water highways, from the interior, came dark-skinned natives in tiny white-sailed dugouts; they lived in mud or palm-leaf huts in villages known only to themselves. Their wants were few—a little food, a little salt, and the indispensable machete— huge knives which serve all purposes from slashing a wide swath through the bush to cutting their tortillas.

The surrounding jungle was a gold mine of orchids. Before long the Indians discovered that so-called weeds meant more to me than food—a brightly colored flowering plant, pulled from its perch on a tree, provided them with twice as much as they received in exchange for a wild turkey or a string of a dozen fish. Crazy, they decided and their disgust was plain to be seen, but they brought plants in ever-increasing numbers. Gradually, I taught them to search for the ones I needed most, especially white orchids, which bring fabulous prices.

Pedro came to me the day before we started back to the coast and said that an old chief, from one of the distant villages, had related to him the story of a gorgeous white orchid he had found; it grew, said he, on a stump above a burial mound. I sent for the Indian at once and eventually bribed him to repeat the tale, but no amount of salt or food or money could induce him to guide me to the spot. He claimed it was near a ruined city, now overgrown with jungle bush. Indians are very superstitious and among them it is a common belief that the spirits of the people who built the city live still in the shadow of the fallen walls.

His description of the orchid, however, convinced me that it was one for which I had long been search- ing, the Lady of the Night, a creamy white species so fragrant when in bloom that it perfumes the jungle for hundreds of feet. But it was not for its beauty or its perfume that I desired it. Certain orchids make better parent plants than others, and this variety was prized by orchid breeders, who used it to secure new hybrids.

Finally, the chief consented to take me up river, as far as the beginning of the trail to the ruined city—farther he would not go. The Duke had gone to the Carib's house for supplies. I hesitated to await his return, as the Indian might become frightened and refuse to go. I left a note, saying we would have

Upper Left: Mayan ruins, Yucatan. *Upper Right:* Foothills of the Andes.
Lower: Banana leaf thatch showing method of overlapping leaves.

Jungle river with wild bananas and heliconias.

to stay over a day; I knew the Professor would understand.

The weather was perfect, the chief in good spirits, and I anticipated no serious difficulties, although it was a bad time for the expedition. The rainy season was nearing its end and, as a result, the banks of the

river were so flooded that no land was to be seen, just stretches of mangrove swamp from which the smell was overpowering. Mosquitoes and insects pumped their poison into me until my hands and face were badly swollen and discolored.

Soon the river became more difficult, filled with snags and fallen trees. I began to look for a clearing where we could camp. Ahead I saw a tiny sand bar running down into the water; brush and trees left an opening apparently wide enough to permit passage of the dugout. The chief swung the boat, never too steady at the best, to one side; it struck the bank with a jolt and we were thrown into the muddy water.

Some time later I found myself lying on the sticky yellow claybank, where the chief had dragged me from the water. Groggy from the effect of the blow, as the boat struck me on the head when it tipped over, I struggled to my feet. All the supplies were a total loss.

I had not noticed that it was rapidly becoming dark. Jagged flashes of lightning illuminated the jungle in a sulphurous glow, followed by a long rumble of thunder that shook the earth beneath us, then the deluge of great, ice-cold drops rattled down from above. The cloudburst assumed the proportions of a giant waterfall, hiding the jungle from our sight, and through a wall of water we made our way along the bank, clinging to the tree roots protruding from its sides.

When the rain slackened we made a fire, using dry inner bark from the trees, and obtained a little relief from the clouds of mosquitoes by standing in the smoke. We kept the fire going all night, piling on huge logs as a protection from wild animals—once we heard the hoarse cough of a prowling jaguar.

Morning came, noon passed, dusk fell. I was shivering with malarial chills and burning with fever; at midnight, when I was more nearly dead than

alive, we heard the sound of a boat. A passing Indian
had seen the reflection of our fire and come to investigate.

I never did get the orchid.

We stood in El Peten in a forest primeval; a forest
of great hardwood trees, whose dignity and antiquity
created an atmosphere very different in character
from that of the swift growth and even swifter
decay of the jungles. The Duke had already made a
survey on foot of a large tract of mahogany; having
selected an acre typical of the entire section, he taped
it off and counted the trees.

It was a magnificent stand. There were few such
left in that region, which has some of the finest red
mahogany in the world. There were hundreds of
trees here, the Duke said; he stood back, squinting
at a superb bole, fully five feet in diameter, taking a
forty-five degree slant at it.

"It's good mahogany," he said, "and will run thousands of feet to the acre. But it's not worth a damn.
We're too far from the Usumacinta to float it out
and it wouldn't pay to jackass it that far. I was
afraid when we came up here that this would be
the case. This country's been too well cruised to over-
look any *easy* bets."

I was glad when I thought that these lovely trees
would perhaps stand like this, unmolested, for years
still to come.

For weeks, by launch and dugout we had followed the river roads into the heart of El Peten. First up the Belize River, which has considerable primitive river traffic, overland past Santo Toribio to the Rio Pasion, and down that tributary of the Usumacinta to the country of the Lacondones.

We traveled through wild country, were wet, cold, hungry. But none of us, I know, will ever forget our experiences. The Professor became interested in Mayan history; the farther we penetrated into their country, the more absorbed he became.

The kingdom of the New Empire of the Mayas, which did not reach its height until A.D. 1000, is infinitely wilder, denser, more menacing than the country of the League of Mayapan in Northern Yucatan, where the ruins of three great cities, Chichen Itza, Mayapan, and Uxmal, still testify to the glories of a civilization decadent while the League was still at its height. In the north of the peninsula there are but a few feet of alluvial soil above the white limestone base of the land. The bush here is light, feathery of foliage, graceful—so graceful that the lack of mountains is scarcely felt.

But toward Petén the surface soil is deeper, the jungles more lush and far more deadly. We were upon the edges of the terrible Petén bush, an impenetrable jungle, great stretches of which no white man has yet succeeded in exploring. There is scarcely a vine, a bush, a tree or a trunk unequipped with thorns. There are curved thorns, daggerlike thorns,

spear-headed thorns, all of which rip the flesh and
pierce right through leather boots and soles.

It is said that Stone-Age tribes still dwell in these
jungle fastnesses. There are tales of survivors of At-
lantis who worship golden calves. But there is no
exaggeration in the stories of the Santa Cruz Indians
who live to the northeast. They are a living survival
of the most bloodthirsty of ancient Mayan peoples.
The Lacondones to the west and south had once possessed a barbaric civilization, in the days when the
Usumacinta was "The Highroad of Nations," and
bore the stream of traffic down from the high plateau
of Mexico, to the great cities of the old Quiche-
Maya empire, Copan, Quirigna, Tikal, Uaxactun.

In the northern part of Yucatan the people must
depend upon wells or cenotes for water; they vary
from fifty to several hundred feet in diameter and
are from thirty to eighty or even one hundred feet
deep. But in Petén there are a number of natural
water holes; some of these the early inhabitants undoubtedly adapted to their needs.

Running through a sunny clearing in the Petén
jungle, the Professor, waving his net as he pursued
a gorgeous butterfly, about fifteen feet in front of
me, suddenly dropped completely from view. There
was not a sound, not a sign of a hole or any place
that could have swallowed him. I was running after
him so fast that I pitched ahead ten or twelve feet
before I could stop; I brought myself up with difficulty on the very brink of one of these natural water

holes, clinging madly to a slender sapling. Peering
over the edge in horror I saw the Professor's bald
head fifteen feet below me, like a pale yellow pumpkin, breaking the surface of the deep, obsidian-black
waters.

He rose up like a cork. I suppose his displacement
in that cisternlike body of water gave additional
buoyancy to his portly anatomy, so that he seemed
to shoot up out of the water. Then he began to swim,
head and shoulders completely above water, with
purposeful directness. He was making towards a tiny
ledge, about thirty feet away at the end of the pool.
I saw at once that the Professor could take care of
himself. He knew how to swim and was giving his
undivided attention to the business of saving himself. His nets floated along behind him; they were
tethered always to his waist.

I ran around the brink of the water hole and
pushed my way through tangled lianas to a spot
where the bank sloped steeply to the little shelving
ledge. There were steps here, ancient steps of carved
sandstone. They led down into the water. I climbed
gingerly down and sat at the foot awaiting the Professor. He came head-on, spouting like a porpoise.
Between each stroke his breast sank down so that
the water came over his chin and he took in great
mouthfuls. Over the top of the dark clear water lay
bright yellow pollen from cascades of orchids and
golden-bell blossoms hanging above the pool. As he

rose with each vigorous stroke, the Professor spouted out his mouthfuls.

"Better keep your mouth closed," I called out to him maliciously. "The Duke says these water holes are full of typhoid germs."

The Professor deflated with alarm, and sank for the moment quite out of sight. Frightened, I reached out for him; but he reappeared to view under the surface at the very foot of the steps and walked like a diver up through the water, apparently from the depths of the hole. We sat on the bottom step while he recovered his breath.

"What did you go and do that for, Professor?" I said seriously. "Dropping out of sight like that, you had me scared for a moment. I did not know where you had gone, or where to look for you. I think that was mean."

He stared at me in reproachful astonishment and then we both burst into roars of laughter. Suddenly he noticed the stone steps upon which we were sitting. "Gott in Himmel!" he exclaimed, "we are at some ruins near."

We climbed the ruined staircase of the well. We followed along an almost obliterated highroad leading westward. It was, literally, a highroad, a sok-bey, raised from two to four feet above the jungle floor and therefore easily distinguished, in spite of the burden of growth covering it. The fernlike trees met in an arch above us, the air was sweet and heavy with shower-of-gold blossoms; suddenly the ruined city lay before us. It was gleaming white in the sunshine, so spotless against the living green of the jungle; oh, the lovely ruined façades of a palace in which once some stocky, skirted nobleman had lived!

Old Empire Maya, Quiche-Maya, for here were none of the signs of Toltec conquest or architecture. We stepped lightly over the grass-covered square and stood at the foot of a small terraced temple with a high carven roof comb. Grass grew from the terrace, roots pried apart the stones of the stairways and the carven pillars, a jungle of trees weighted the already massive roots. Little monkeys, green parrokeets— love birds—cheeped and chittered as they swung through the dank steep-pitched chambers. This city probably was found by archaeologists years ago; some hand had cleared away the debris from the altar, some hand had restored a tiny part of its beauty.

The Duke had told me that the Maya cities looked like the ruins of Cambodia, of Angkor Wat and Angkor Thom. But I was not prepared for this. We stayed a long time, the Professor and I, until a gusano fly bit the Professor in the neck. Fortunately I saw it just as, having deposited its egg in the back of his neck, it soared away. I immediately dug out the little red spot with my penknife, so the Professor wouldn't have a worm, and poured some good strong iodine in the small cut.

"Lucky it wasn't a doctor fly," I cheered him; the Tabanus poison causes terrible swelling and an inflammation which is very painful.

The Duke, the Professor, and the Doctor, with most of the equipment, went down the Usumacinta to Tenosique. Bitten by orchid fever, I stayed behind for a few days to finish some paintings for a one-man show I wanted to hold in New York; I kept two reliable men with me. The Duke fussed about it for a while, but, on my promise to be careful, gave in.

I hated to see them go. The jungle was very quiet, very lonely, after their huge dugout, hollowed from a thirty-foot mahogany log, drifted down the stream and around a bend.

Everything went wrong after that!

Wishing to meet and see at close hand some of the treacherous Lacondones, really Mayas, is one thing, but literally to stumble upon one of their camping places is quite another.

We had crossed the upper Lacantun and were making our way slowly through the thick virgin jungle, keeping a close lookout for snakes, when Quin, the guide who was leading, parted some creepers with his machete. We found ourselves almost in the middle of a Lacondones village, built on the bank of a tiny stream, if three huts can be called a village. Entering by the back door, so to speak, had taken them entirely by surprise; their front entrance is well-guarded, with pitfalls and poisoned trails. Snake venom or other deadly poison is rubbed on thorns and an unsuspecting person, approaching, rubs against them and is thus killed.

The women melted into the bush without a sound,

but not before I glimpsed their straggly, unkempt hair, the filthy garments, like a poncho, that reached only to their knees and was their only covering. The men had no time to run, being closer to us when we came out of the jungle; they looked even more degenerate than the women.

There were few attractions about this place, but having stumbled upon it, we decided to stay the night and make friends with the natives if we could. We picked out the cleanest of the huts—a mere bunch of poles draped with leaves, without even mud stuffed in the cracks of the sticks—and moved in. The men eyed us curiously, but made no move of any sort. Tiny gardens, cleared by burning off the jungle, were planted to the very doors of the dwellings with maize, tobacco, native cotton from which they made their one-piece garments, and quantities of pumpkins—the dried shells of these last they used as drinking and eating utensils.

Gradually the women drifted back into the clearing; there were three men at home, the others, Quin said, were fishing. Late that night they returned, bringing a large catch in their crude hollowed-out canoe; the fish had all been shot with feather-tipped bamboo arrows from the back of the boat. The bows were crudely formed, but mighty effective; the poison is a combination of snake venom and the sap from a liana.

I made large and handsome presents of the thing for which they would sell their souls—salt. It was a

mistake. They decided to keep with them perma-
nently such marvelous gods, who could apparently
produce their necessities at will. Still believing in
white gods, the Lacondones would not, I think, harm
white people unless they thought them spies, or unless they tried to get away. The largest, most degenerate of them, who probably was their chief, answered to the name of Chen Tonn (the best I can
spell it). He camped outside the hut in which I was
living and fastened to the frame two of the most
beautiful ocelots I have ever seen. Their liana leash
was just long enough so that they roamed back and
forth before the entrance; it was not until I reached
Tenosique that I discovered that Indians train these
cats to hunt deer or other game. I could have walked
right past them without the slightest harm. Unfortunately, I didn't know it.

I did nothing about it for two days, simply because I didn't know what to do; then I got to thinking how the Duke would worry if I didn't show up
very soon. Malaria returned and for a day or so I
didn't have to worry about anything; a fever of 104
degrees leaves one no time to fret. That was the night
the scorpion stung me.

Every night I wrapped myself up snugly in an
elaborate headdress of mosquito netting, tied snugly
around my neck, terrified of the insects which
crawled all over the thatch, the earth floor, and even
over the vegetation around the clearing. For all I
knew, some of them might be the terrible insects that

lays eggs in the nose and ear of a sleeper; the hatched
maggots cause a frightful death. Somehow, I never
thought to be afraid of the spiders. It was my outthrust elbow that proved an Achilles' heel. They had
taken away my hammock and Quin, whom they
would not allow near me, shouted that the others
had been stolen by his helper, who had taken advantage of the opportunity to run away with everything
he could get his hands upon.

During my fevered tossing from side to side on
my blanket, spread upon the dirty earthen floor, a
scorpion dropped from the thatch upon my arm; apparently I tried to brush it off, for it struck, deep,
so deep that I had to pull the stinger out with my
fingers. For days my right arm was paralyzed from
the shoulder to the wrist; the poison did something
peculiar also to my throat, for I could scarcely swal-
low liquid. Great sores broke out upon the arm and
would not heal. Weeks after my return to the States,
a horrible, running wound still remained. Finally, Dr.
Ditmars, Curator of reptiles of the New York Zoo,
being consulted, said that a poultice of laundry soap
might be tried; it did the trick—the sores healed up
in a week, but I still have no feeling in the place
where the sting penetrated.

Finally, when I had recovered sufficiently to travel,
Quin crawled up to the back of my hut on a pitch-
black night and cut away, with his machete, the
sticks which formed its framework. I crawled out
of the hole, like a heroine in a "thriller", leaving one

blanket on the floor, in case Chen Tonn came looking
for his "salt". Quin, being Mayan, could travel in
the dark as though it were daylight, but I was not
so lucky. Further, I had no idea where their trails
lay; at any minute one of us might be impaled upon
a poisoned thorn, or they might discover our absence
and decide to follow us, although that seemed to me
unlikely. We made directly for the riverbank, traveling lightly and swiftly, to put as much distance as
possible between us and the Lacondones by daybreak.

Quin said a short way below where he expected to
strike the river, he had seen a small canoe, in which
we could reach Tenosique. The dark held for me
innumerable terrors, for every time a branch moved
I thought it was the Lacondones creeping through
the bush. The night was very still; not even the
frogs, it seemed, dared to croak if the natives were
astir. The trees shed moisture constantly; my shirt
was soaked through before we had gone ten yards.

I was exhausted, but Quin urged me on with
boosts, prayers, and something—some muttered jar-
gon that I imagine was curses. The air was getting
frightfully hot; I looked over my shoulder and a
great scarlet blaze filled the heavens. Tongues of
flame leaped from tree to tree, from clump of dried
grass to dried grass; in spite of the heavy dew, the
jungle will burn. Little sparks began to flicker before
my eyes. This was the end. I could go no further.
The sparks were not my eyes—the bushes ahead of
us were on fire. I caught my boot in a creeper, fell

headlong; rolled down the bank and into the shallows along the river margin.

Stumbling and floundering through the shallows we reached the canoe and piled in. Quin made for the middle of the river; his vigorous paddling, aided by the swift current, soon carried us far down the stream, away from the breath of the forest fire, from the menace of Lacondon trails and Lacondon poison.

Quin paddled at night, keeping well in midstream, while I slept, rolled in my blanket in the bottom of the dugout. By day we tied up to the bank in some sheltered spot. It took three days to go down the broad, dark Usumacinta to Tenosique. We rode without mishap the wide swift current where for centuries Aztec traders, Mayan merchant princes, warriors and slaves, had passed to and from Texcoco's shores to the rich cities of the Coclé in Panama.

Today there is but one real town upon the upper Usumacinta—tiny Tenosique. How glad I was to see its pretty, grassy little streets, the whitewashed houses, clean and fresh on the high sunny bank above us.

Chapter Sixteen

THE END OF THE TRAIL

Tenosique—River canoa—Start for home—Call of the jungle

HIGH ABOVE THE jungle rode the waxing moon. It cast its ghostly mantle of white light over the landscape and changed the same world of the living to a phantom world; giant creepers and twisted branches etched their snaky silhouette across its golden face. Like a river of oil the Usumacinta flowed between walls of dense, impenetrable hardwoods along its banks; no breeze ruffled the black, calm surface of its waters. The night air was chill, damp. But I stretched out contentedly in a hammock on the deck on the canoa. For the first time in weeks I was really cool.

The Duke, busy transferring our equipment from a wattle-and-mud hut in Tenosique, the outpost of civilization, hove into sight and paused to ask how I felt.

"Fine," I assured him and he started back with the porters for another load.

A husky, blond planter settled himself in a chair near by. He noticed my bandaged arm and sling.

"Accident?" he asked.

"No. Scorpion."

"Great Scott! Wonder you didn't die. Going home now?" His voice was wistful.

"Yes." I shut my eyes and the planter went away.

I could hear the pat-pat-pat of Indian women making tortillas; the scrape of many feet on hard-packed floors; and always laughter. I could smell the fragrance of chocolate, vanilla, and orange and scarlet blossoms, the smell of overripe bananas, and the smell of good earth dampened by the afternoon's rain. Flares lighted up grassy streets as the Duke started down the steep bank with the last load.

The boat pushed off as I made my way over the deck, where a few natives already were lying asleep, wrapped in their ragged blankets. Most of them were bound for Villa Hermosa, but the others we would take with us to Frontera, the port for the fertile fruit, chicle, and lumber regions of northern Guatemala, Chiapas, and Tobasco.

The Duke had made our beds on the deck. Long after his deep breathing told me he was fast asleep, I lay watching the great moon that threaded thin fingers of pale silver between massive clumps of palm and bamboo.

The long trips, the hardships, the excitement, all were over. We were going home.

A poor-me-one flew low above me. Its eyes glowed in the light burning on the deck below. Its plaintive call sounded from the jungle, as though begging me to answer.

Sometime, in the future, I shall answer. I will go back—back to the silence and the magic of the jungle, back to the flowers, the beasts and the birds. But Matéo will not be there. Already he has become a memory, a voice from the past. And if I find no other simple soul as loyal, I will have to walk, like Kipling's cat, alone.

GRASS HUT COOKERY

GRASS HUT COOKERY

"THE CULTURE of a country," say the Latins, "can be judged by its kitchens."

Latin America is a gourmet's paradise. Even Nero Wolfe would crave its national dishes, as well as its orchids. Together with a liking for the land, I inherited from my ancestors an equal liking for good food. In the cities of South and Central America, I collected recipes as another person might collect old furniture. In the jungles we were forced often to substitute certain ingredients but in many cases this added to the piquancy of the flavor or actually compounded a new dish more palatable than the old one.

The following recipes are those for which all the ingredients may be obtained readily in this country. There is little or no difference in the ingredients used in foreign cooking; the difference lies in the strange combinations of these foods.

Olla Podrida

1 pound of mutton, cubed	2 bay leaves
1 pound of beef, cubed	1 pimiento
1 small stewing chicken	3 large ripe tomatoes, quartered
1 clove of garlic, minced	tered
2 large onions, finely cut	Salt
1 dozen ripe olives	$\frac{1}{2}$ cup salt pork, chopped fine
1 green sweet pepper, chopped	

Cut up chicken. Put in large kettle and cover with water. Sear cubed mutton and beef in hot fat, in iron skillet, until lightly browned and add to chicken. Cover and cook five minutes. Add salt, bay leaf, and salt pork. Cook slowly until meat is nearly tender (about fifteen minutes), adding more water if required. Add balance of ingredients and cook thirty minutes or until done. Season to taste. Approximate yield: 8 portions.

Cervo Asado

5 pounds of venison
Bacon
1 cup of sour cream

1 cup of hot water
¼ pound of butter

Lard venison with bacon and rub with garlic if desired. Put in deep roasting pan on trivet. Melt butter and pour over venison. Sear quickly in hot oven for ten minutes; reduce heat to moderate. Roast, allowing fifteen minutes per pound, basting occasionally. Remove roast to hot platter. Add sour cream and hot water to drippings in pan. Thicken with flour and cook slowly on top of stove, stirring to blend gravy. Season to taste.

Riñoncito al Vino

6 small lamb kidneys
2 large tomatoes
1 large onion, thinly sliced
¼ cup Sherry or Madeira

¼ cup of olive oil
1 teaspoonful of salt
¼ teaspoonful of pepper

Skin and split kidneys. Season, dip in olive oil, and arrange on skewers with alternate slices of onion and tomato. Broil fifteen minutes under high flame, turning frequently. Place on hot platter, pour wine over and serve with buttered toast.

Pavo del Monte

1 8-10 pound turkey	2 sections of garlic
½ pound salt pork	2 tablespoonfuls of butter
1 hot green pepper (or chili powder)	Salt
	Wild rice stuffing
6 large tomatoes	

Sprinkle cleaned and dried bird with salt, inside and out. Fill loosely with prepared rice stuffing and sew opening. Slice pork and lay over entire breast of bird. Place in roasting pan, add pepper sauce (Recipe following) and bake in hot oven until bird is tender, basting with the sauce about every twenty minutes.

Wild rice stuffing

2 cups wild rice	1 cup tomato juice
½ cup olive oil	1 cup meat stock
1 medium onion, chopped	Salt and pepper
1 egg, beaten	

Wash and dry rice. Heat oil in frying pan. Add rice and onion; cook until onion is well-browned. Add tomato juice, meat stock, and seasoning, then stir in egg. Cook slowly about thirty minutes. Approximately seven cups of stuffing.

Hot pepper sauce: melt two tablespoons of butter in frying pan. Brown garlic and chopped green pepper until soft. Add 1 cup of hot water, salt to taste, and 6 minced tomatoes. Cook until done and add to turkey for basting.

This stuffing and basting sauce can be used also for duck or any game. In the tropics, sliced or quartered oranges are served often with roasted game or meats.

Panqueque

1 cup white flour	6 eggs
⅔ cup milk	Salt

Make thin batter of milk and flour. Add eggs, one at a time, and beat briskly. Pinch of salt. Melt tablespoonful of butter in frying pan; when hot, pour in a sixth portion of batter and fry evenly on both sides to a golden brown. Serve these pancakes with honey or jam.

Flan

½ cup orange juice	¼ cup brandy
½ cup pineapple juice	½ cup sugar
5 eggs well beaten	

Combine fruit juice and half of the sugar; bring to boil and then cool. Add eggs and brandy. Stir well. Caramelize balance of sugar in top of double boiler. Pour into caramelized sugar the eggs, brandy and fruit juices. Cook slowly over hot water until thick. Turn out into dessert dish to cool. This recipe serves six persons.

Acknowledgments and Recommendations

ALTHOUGH this is a book based solely on personal experience, I have read the works of many authors on Latin America, in order to note any changes in town or places since I visited those countries; also I consulted these same authorities to check and verify certain facts of history, natural history, and ethnology. I wish, therefore, to express my sincere thanks and acknowledge my indebtedness to the following persons: McFee, Beals, Franck, Beebe, Seton, Fleming, Duguid, Tschiffely, Miller, Roosevelt, Zahm, Guenther, Desmond, Simmons, Gann, Verrill, Childers, Freeman, Forbes, Gibson, Thompson, Murphy, Chapman, Nordang, Wardlaw, Ullman, Russell, Strode, Bowman-Dickinson, Deuel, Halle, de Prorok, Rusby, Loederer, Mitchell-Hedges, Ditmars, and Cunningham Grahame, whom it was Matéo's boast to call friend. The books of these authors provide a remarkable cross-section of the Latin America of today. I further recommend books by Darwin, Humboldt, Bates, Wallace, Spruce, Prescott, Hudson, Herring, Waldo Frank, Bryce, and Tomlinson.

I am deeply grateful for the favors of my many kind friends in Central and South America, but space does not permit me to list them. I wish especially, however, to thank General Rondon for valuable information and the use of maps, the Farquer Syndicate for innumerable kindnesses, and the physicians attached to the Rockefeller Foundation Commission for advice regarding sanitary and health precautions.

In North America I am indebted to the following persons for various favors: Mary Bray, Alida Malkus, Helen Harrington, and Neal and John Townley. For help in the taking or securing of a few of the pictures I wish to thank Nancy Searle and Paul Paddock, who were with me in Mexico, Isabelle Romans and E. Buechler of Casa Grace, La Paz. The picture of the jungle river is by Hugo Brehme; the one of the solid-wheel cart is by courtesy of the Minister of the Interior, Chile. Source material for the mythological figure on the large map was an astronomical map by George Annand and a map of the constellations published in *The Story of the Stars* by J. D. Steele, 1884.

Mr. Milton Trindade, of the Brazilian Information Bureau, to whom I submitted the section of manuscript on Brazil, supplied me with official maps of his country and verified for me various records. To him I owe especial thanks for his kindness. Through the courtesy of the Brazilian Information Bureau I was permitted to use the following photographs: those of Sasha Siemel, opposite pages 111 (*lower*), 158 (*lower*), 159 (*lower*), 222 (*lower*); those of Senhor Silva Jr., opposite pages 31 (*lower*),

94 (*lower*), 110, 175, 206 (*lower*) ; and those of Colleccão Panair, opposite pages 30 (*lower*) and 206 (*upper*).   To each of these gentlemen I offer my sincere thanks.

7-23-39